DATE DUE

OC 6 '92			
FE 0 '9			
FE 22 9			
JE 17 '9			
SE 10 '9			
OC 1 '9			
OC 15 '9			
FE 2 '94			
4/24/09			

THE
COMMUNIST
MANIFESTO

Manifest

der

Kommunistischen Partei.

Veröffentlicht im Februar 1848.

Proletarier aller Länder vereinigt euch.

London.

Gedruckt in der Office der „Bildungs=Gesellschaft für Arbeiter"
von J. E. Burghard
46, Liverpool Street, Bishopsgate.

Cover of the First Edition of the Manifesto.

THE
COMMUNIST
MANIFESTO

KARL MARX
and FRIEDRICH ENGELS

The revolutionary economic,
political, and social treatise
that has transfigured the world

Amereon House
Mattituck

THE COMMUNIST MANIFESTO

Reprinted 1977 by Special Arrangement

The first edition of the *Communist Manifesto* was published in German in 1848 by J. E. Burghard, London.

TO THE READER

It is our pleasure to keep available uncommon titles and to this end, at the time of publication, we have used the best available sources. To aid catalogers and collectors, this title is printed in an edition limited to 300 copies.

——— **Enjoy!**

To order contact
AMEREON HOUSE, the publishing division of Amereon Ltd.
Postal Box 1200
Mattituck, New York 11952

The Communist Manifesto
ISBN 0-89190-549-9

Manufactured in the United States of America

Contents

Introduction
Marx the Romantic

COMMUNISTS in all parts of the world proclaim that all of their actions are logically derived from the teachings of Lenin, who, they believe, built in turn on the doctrines of Marx and Engels. Communists insist that communism was born in the mind of Karl Marx in the middle of the nineteenth century, and that it received its first definitive expression in 1848 when Marx, with the help of Friedrich Engels, published what has come to be the most famous pamphlet in the history of the world, *The Communist Manifesto*.

We tend to think of Marx and Engels as fierce old men with piles of white hair and bushy beards, whose huge disembodied heads are painted on giant red banners borne aloft by faceless thousands of marching men through the streets of a totalitarian capital, carried between tanks and missiles and pictures of the current dictator as part of some revolutionary celebration in some vast militarized state. In fact, when Marx and Engels wrote *The Com-*

7

Introduction

munist Manifesto they were unknown young men in their late twenties, whose beards were not yet bushy, whose hair was not yet in the least white, who despised soldiers, and who hated all despotic states.

Early in 1848 there were no communist states in the world and no revolutionary governments of any sort. There was no Communist party in our sense and no revolutionary organizations or even trade unions of any size. A few countries of northwest Europe and a few areas of the United States were industrializing rapidly, but there was no city in the world—even London—much bigger than two million people, and no state—even Great Britain—in which a majority of the people did not live in the country and farm for a living. Every country in the world—except the Americas and Switzerland—was a monarchy of some sort, and in most of them the king, emperor, tsar, or sultan ruled absolutely and without any formal check. Even in free America there were millions of slaves, and even in free Great Britain most men were too poor to qualify for the vote. No woman in the civilized world—save possibly Queen Victoria—was fully and legally free from control by father, husband, or some other man. Every country was what we would now call "backward," and way over ninety per cent of the world's population lived in what we would call horrible and unendurable poverty—1848 was very long ago.

Into this now vanished world Karl Marx was born in 1818, in the western German city of Treves (Trier), which still boasts of the finest Roman ruins in northern Europe. Treves then belonged to Prussia, the second most powerful of the many independent German states, and the most efficient reactionary police tyranny in Europe. Marx always detested the Prussian regime. He renounced his Prussian citizenship while still in his twenties, and spent most of his life in exile, wanted by the Prussian police.

The Marxes were a Jewish family; both father and mother had come from families of rabbis. But Marx's father, educated in the anti-religious atmosphere of the late eighteenth-century Enlightenment, gave up Judaism and the Jewish community, and became a lawyer and a Prussian official. Eventually, when Karl Marx was six, his father had himself and his whole family baptized as Lutherans not because he admired Luther or believed in Jesus, but to save his career in what was officially Lutheran Prussia, although Treves itself was a Catholic city.

An enormous amount of nonsense has been written about Marx because he was born into a Jewish family. He was never taught much about Judaism or Jewish life, and he was proud of his ignorance. He was often twitted and sneered at in his youth for being Jewish, but he never suffered much when he was young or later from the prevailing anti-Semitism, either in his career, or, so far as we can tell, in his psyche. He had few Jewish friends. He wrote a fair amount about the Jews of Europe, always regarding Judaism as a stupid superstition, and the Jews as a community caught in the vise of capitalism from which only the revolution could free them. He adopted from his Christian neighbors the habit of calling ideas and people he did not like "dirty-Jewish" whether they were Jewish or not, and when he really hated someone (for instance, Ferdinand Lassalle, a man of Jewish origin who became the greatest German socialist and trade union leader in the 1860's), Marx would call him a "dirty Jew of Negro blood." Marx was not really a Jew. Hitler thought that communism was one vast Jewish plot, citing as proof the "fact" that Marx was Jewish. But Hitler was crazy, and other anti-Communists would do well to avoid this mode of thought.

Other kinds of nonsense are written by people who know that Marx, in spite of his family background, was not really Jewish. One often reads that Marx was cut off from European society by being Jewish, and from Jewish society by no longer being Jewish, and that he was able to fathom the future socialist society because he was thus alienated from his own. One often reads that Marx had the moral indignation of a Hebrew prophet because of his Jewish background, that he was concerned with human happiness in this world rather than in the next because of his Jewish background, and that he was given to fierce self-righteousness, absolute dogmatism, and violent abusiveness because of his Jewish background. People who believe such things are usually at a loss to explain why most denouncers of the evils of early industrialism were of Christian origin, as were most socialists, and why most Christian intellectuals of the day also expressed themselves in strong terms. Marx was far outdone in alienation, in wrathful denunciation, and in dogmatic abusiveness by such sons of Christian noblemen as Mikhail Bakunin and Vladimir Lenin. Marx's Jewish background is not the key to Marx.

Marx's father wanted his son to become a lawyer like himself, and sent him through the best schools in Treves, and then, in 1835, to study law at the University of Bonn. The University was something of a country club, and young Marx joined the other students in drinking, brawling, scarring each other in dueling games, piling up debts, and joining "subversive" (*i.e.,* politically liberal) clubs. Old Marx in disgust transferred his son to the University of Berlin, which had a justified reputation for a more intellectual faculty and student body—much as an American father, a generation ago, might have transferred his son from Princeton or Williams to Columbia. By and large, it worked. Young Marx stayed at Berlin until 1841, studying law and philosophy, and he became as heavy an intellectual as any father could have wished. In one respect it did not work. Young Marx became increasingly and incurably subversive, but his father died in 1838 before he became fully aware of his son's political bent.

The intellectual world in which Marx formed his mind was one of the most complicated of any in the history of humanity. Marx belonged to the third generation of the great Romantic current in European thought and culture. Romanticism, like the other important abstract nouns in the history of culture, is not a term to be defined but a field to be explored. To most Americans today, the word "romantic" implies sentimental love stories and swashbuckling adventure tales of the Hollywood type. There were plenty of those in the Romantic age, but the term is used by historians in many broader senses. A grim realistic novel by Balzac was just as Romantic in its way as a romance by Sir Walter Scott. There were Romantic plays and poems as well as stories, Romantic painting and sculpture, Romantic architecture and music—all familiar enough. But there were also Romantic politics, Romantic history, Romantic religion, Romantic philosophy, and Romantic science—in fact, every human activity could be conducted Romantically.

It is difficult to find anything common to all the aspects of late eighteenth- and nineteenth-century European (and American) culture that historians call Romantic. A great deal of Romanticism involved the cultivation of human emotions, especially love, but also exalted joy and profound melancholy, youthful protest, delight in struggle, artistic sensibility, and many more. On public questions, a Romantic might pursue a liberal or radical course inspired by the French Revolution, or he might react conservatively against it. In either case, he would probably be much concerned with his people or nation, its characteristics, its history, its folklore and folk arts. In the natural sciences or the social sciences, a Romantic would usually be concerned with tracing the history, development, and progress of the stars, the earth, plants and animals, man, a nation, a social institution—in short, he would be concerned with *evolution,* one of the key Romantic ideas. Romantic philosophers often emphasized the evolution of the world and human society. Many Romantics participated in the revival of religion in the early nineteenth century, usually a private and emotional religion. In the arts and in literature, Romantics usually reacted against the many rules and restraints of the French Classical culture of the seventeenth and eighteenth centuries in favor of their own national traditions, of freer forms, and of greater emotional expression.

Most Romantics were concerned with some small individual part of the world, a poet with some of his own emotions, a scientist with a few specimens in his laboratory, but the more ambitious Romantics tried to build up vast philosophical or scientific systems to describe the evolution of the universe and the nature of man (e.g., Hegel's philosophy), or vast artistic syntheses to express the emotional life and predicament of man (e.g., Wagner's operas). Obviously no one Romantic personality could combine all the currents mentioned above in himself, least of all Marx. The mature Marx would have angrily denied that he was a Romantic, for he used the term in a narrower sense to denote and abuse a number of emotional, religious, and mushy-headed men he despised. He called himself a scientific philosopher and a scientific socialist. For all that, it is fair and useful to call Marx's science, philosophy, and socialism a Romantic science, philosophy, and socialism. Marx was the greatest of the high Romantic ideologists of the mid-nineteenth century, just as his contemporary, Wagner, was the greatest of the high Romantic composers, and just as another contemporary, Darwin, was the greatest of the high Romantic scientists. Marxists would still deny this heatedly, but a less partisan observer can perhaps see that Marx will always be misunderstood unless he is set against the background of his own Europe of the high Romantic age.

In his years at the University of Berlin, Marx became imbued with the following convictions that were not necessarily Romantic in themselves, but which, taken together, and taken in the peculiar emotional way of young men in Marx's day *were* Romantic: He came to believe that all the various sciences and philosophies were part of one overarching system, which, when completed, would give a true and total picture of the universe and man. (The Romantics had transformed this faith, which they had inherited from their scientific predecessors.) He came to believe that the core of such a science and philosophy was the growth, development, progress, and evolution of the world, human society, and the individual, particularly the mechanism by which such evolution took place. He came to believe that nature and man evolve according to certain inexorable scientific laws, whose working out can be embodied but not opposed by even the greatest men, such as Napoleon. Marx and his fellow students found the most thorough statement of these views in the works of the then recently deceased philosopher, Georg Wilhelm Friedrich Hegel, but they were by no means all straightforward disciples of Hegel.

Unlike Hegel, Marx came to believe that there was no God. He even spent some time trying vainly to prove that Hegel had also been an atheist. He became sure that Europe was trembling on the edge of reaction and revolution, that existing societies were dark, cruel, tense, and unstable, and that most of mankind was ground down, unhappy, of divided mind, disaffected from society, and cut off from its own true nature. This was the unfortunate condition that Marx and his contemporaries called man's *alienation.* Such convictions were a variety of radical Romanticism, which in the Germanies was called Left Hegelianism.

Having become a radical, Marx was in no mood to take up the practice of law in reactionary Prussia when he left the University of Berlin. Instead, he became a radical journalist. Early in 1842 he joined the staff of a liberal newspaper in Cologne, the *Rheinische Zeitung.* By the end of the year the twenty-four-year-old Marx was made editor-in-chief. Five months later, in 1843, the radicalism and venom of Marx's editorials provoked the Prussian police into suppressing the whole paper. At this point Marx finally got around to marrying his fiancée of long standing, Jenny von Westphalen, a childhood neighbor of his in Treves, who came from a family of Lutheran officials and was four years older than himself. The couple moved from their homeland forever, first to Paris for four years, where Marx tried not very successfully to make a living at journalism and other writing.

During 1843 and 1844, Marx was acquiring, through his reading, another set of convictions that was to be crucial to his future doctrine. He was absorbing the books of Malthus, Ricardo, and other British economists of the earlier Romantic period. Marx accepted much of their economic analysis, but disagreed wholly with their Romantic pessimism and their Romantic reactionary political judgments of the workingmen. Instead, Marx was led to choose the industrial workingmen (for whom he adopted, Romantically, a term out of ancient Roman history, the "proletarians") as the key to the future development of society, as the great Romantic cause of his life.

In the last generation, scholars such as Professor Sidney Hook of New York University and Professor Leonard Krieger of Yale have shown that Marx's ideas during 1843 and 1844 were exceedingly interesting and complex, and much more broad-minded and attractive to our ways of thinking than his later dogmatic obsession with proletarian revolution. More recently a New York psychoanalyst named Erich Fromm has written a curious and unconvincing book on Marx that has dwelt on this early period in an attempt to show that Marx was really a kind of existentialist sage like his Danish contemporary Kierkegaard, and that Marx was chiefly concerned with the sick divided souls of men, with their revulsion and alienation from their work and their lives. Marx, in this view, hit on revolution chiefly as a therapeutic means to heal the sick souls of the working class and the rest of humanity. If this is so, then the world has been long deceived.

By the end of 1844, Marx had established his lifelong friendship with Friedrich Engels. Engels was born in 1820 in Barmen, Prussia, a town just south of the then developing industrial district of the Ruhr. His father, a tyrannical Calvinist, was a manufacturer who owned cotton mills near the Ruhr and in England. Young Engels became converted to radicalism during a brief stay at the University of Berlin in 1841. His father at once dispatched him to England to learn the textile business. Engels learned it, and with it he learned of the grim life led by English workers in the early days of the industrial revolution. He also acquired an Irish factory girl, Mary Burns, as a mistress. He never married, but stayed with her over twenty years until her death. Engels' relationship to Mary Burns, during the height of the Victorian age, alienated him from society far more than communism could have. Since

Introduction

Marx and Engels discussed all projects together, even when they did not actually write a piece together, it is often hard to sort out their respective contributions. But everyone, starting with Engels himself, has judged that Marx had the more striking and original mind of the two.

During the middle 1840's, Marx and/or Engels produced a number of works in which they depicted the ghastly condition of the growing working class, engaged in vigorous debates with other radicals, and began to set forth their own version of what they called "communism" in the 1840's, which has usually been called "socialism" since 1850. Today one can usually tell the difference between the Socialist and Communist parties of any given country. Although attempts have been made to distinguish between socialism with a small *s* and communism with a small *c*—often by saving the term "communism" to indicate a more radical, more violent, or more evolved stage of "socialism"—the two words have usually been used overlappingly if not interchangeably. Attempts at formal definition, such as the old chestnut that "socialism is the public ownership of means of production, distribution, and exchange," break up on the rocks of divergent common usage.

No matter what the definition, it is clear that the socialist movement arose in the Romantic age, and

19

is one of the major Romantic legacies to the twentieth century. The hundreds of millions of people who have called themselves Socialists and/or Communists have all believed that the system of private property they knew—whether it was in industrial capital, piles of money, landed estates, serfs, or slaves—was wrong, and that the consequent inequality between the rich and the poor was wrong, and that any exploitation of one human being by another was wrong. This highly Romantic sense of social wrong, and the consequent highly Romantic drive toward social justice, which Marx and Engels shared to a high degree, are the ethical and emotional bases of any socialist movement.

Virtually all socialists have subscribed to a characteristically Romantic solution to these social problems: to end all or much private property; to turn the land, the factories, and the banks, at least, over to the community. Beyond these essentials, socialists disagree among themselves. There is a clear distinction between the religious socialists and the atheist socialists, who are the majority. There is another clear distinction between socialists who want to accomplish their aims by peaceful political means, and those who are willing to engage in violent revolution. Some socialists want to turn private property over to national or international governments; others (including most Russian socialists up to 1917) want to turn private property over to small decentralized social units, co-operatives or village communes. Some socialists want to establish a libertarian democracy soon after the revolution; others insist on a long period of dictatorship for the sake of political consolidation and economic buildup.

Marx and Engels were atheist socialists who urged violent revolution to be followed by a brief "dictatorship of the proletariat" in the course of which much private property would be turned over to the government. Marx furthermore insisted that his was the only *scientific* socialism, based not on wishful thinking but on the inexorable laws of nature and history, which would drive men toward socialism no matter what anybody or everybody thought, felt, or did. These classifications are difficult because almost all socialist groups take their doctrines so seriously that they deny the name of socialism—and all honorable intention—to all rival socialist groups.

In 1847, while Marx was calling most other socialist thinkers in Europe "dirty Jews of Negro blood," he was kicked out of Paris and France by the French police, in order to please the Prussian police. He moved to Brussels, and then to London to join Engels. Throughout the 1840's they had been involved with one or another miniscule group of socialist intellectuals and/or workingmen. In 1847

they were most interested in the Communist
League, an allegedly international group of workingmen, chiefly composed of exiled German intellectuals. They attended a minute congress of this
League in London in November, 1847—indeed
they dominated it. They had themselves commissioned to draw up a complete theoretical and practical party program. The Communist League lasted
only long enough to see some of its members rail-
roaded to prison in 1852 by the Prussian police.
But the program of Marx and Engels, which was
printed in German and published February, 1848,
in London, has survived as the first definitive statement of their variety of socialism. Their program—
The Communist Manifesto—has become the most
widely read and influential pamphlet in the history
of the world.

The Communist Manifesto was allegedly addressed to the workingmen of the world (by which
Marx and Engels meant Europe). In fact, it seems
to be addressed as much if not more to educated
middle-class people who rejected communism; there
are whole pages of argument directed to such people. Today it is read mainly by students. In communist countries the pamphlet is read in all the
schools; in America it is read in college courses on

Introduction

European history, economics, and Western civilization. To most American students it seems windy and rhetorical in style, and simultaneously radical and old-fashioned in substance. The argument can hardly have converted any American to socialism for decades. At this late date, it is wholly "non-subversive"!

Marx and Engels began with the famous sentence, "A specter is haunting Europe—the specter of communism." Nowadays this makes most people smile because it is true today as it never was in 1848, but with a wholly different meaning. At the beginning of 1848, the tsar of Russia and his fellow rulers feared a revolution, but it was a liberal revolution by the middle classes they feared, not a socialist revolution by the workingmen. Marx and Engels Romantically exaggerated the importance of their movement.

The Communist Manifesto is divided into four chapters of decreasing importance. The first chapter, "Bourgeois and Proletarians," is crucial. There are a number of ways of sub-dividing humanity—by sexes, by age groups, by religions, etc. The most characteristic Romantic way to sub-divide humanity was into nations. Most Romantic thinkers were nationalists to some degree; they were much concerned with their own nation, or people, a group that usually shared a common territory, language, religion, culture, and history. If the people had already been unified into a common nation-state—as the English, French, and Russians had—a nationalist was concerned with the past and present glories of the state, and with strengthening and perfecting the unity of the people. If the people had not yet been unified—as the Germans and the Italians had not—or if they were occupied by foreign powers—as the Irish and Poles were—a nationalist was concerned with the past glories of his people, and with political campaigns to expel the foreigners and unify the country. Nationalists tended to play down the class divisions within a people in the interest of national unity. These nationalist movements were very widespread and deep in Romantic Europe. Nationalist sentiment has been a major legacy of the Romantic age to the later Europe of the two World Wars, and to all the backward and colonial peoples of the world.

It is therefore amazing that Marx and Engels, who lived right in the middle of it all, not only failed to share the nationalist feelings of their fellow Germans, but failed to recognize the force of Romantic nationalism in others. "The workingmen have no country," they wrote in *The Communist Manifesto*. "National differences and antagonisms are vanishing gradually from day to day, owing to the development of the bourgeoisie, to freedom of commerce,

24

to the world market. . . ." This was flatly false, more obviously and stupidly false than anything else in Marx's whole doctrine. On the eve of the revolutions of 1848, a titanic set of nationalist explosions, Marx judged that national feeling was on the way out. At the beginning of a hundred-year period in which workingmen were to become increasingly swept up by nationalist feelings, Marx declared that they had no country.

Marx's feelings, but not Marx's blindness, are explained by the fact that he and many other socialists divided humanity in another characteristically Romantic way, into social classes. At a time when most European countries were still ruled, or at least co-ruled, by kings and nobles, Marx had the vision to see that the bourgeoisie was taking over. "Bourgeoisie" had originally meant the inhabitants of cities, but by the Romantic age the term had come to mean the middle classes, whether they lived in cities or not. Businessmen from the greatest textile magnates to the smallest hole-in-the-wall shopkeepers, doctors, lawyers, teachers and other educated and professional people, all the groups that we now call "white collar workers" were part of the bourgeoisie. Marx often felt compelled to give a narrow economic definition of the bourgeoisie— "the owners of the means of capitalist production"

—but he used the term to indicate the middle classes as a whole.

The proletarians had originally been the poverty stricken masses of ancient Rome, who had no property save their children (*proles*). The Roman poor had nothing whatsoever to do with factories, but Marx took over the term for modern factory workers because he liked its grand Romantic historical sweep. In spite of his formal economic definitions, Marx usually included all the urban poor in the proletarians, whether they worked in factories or not. He was convinced that with the evolution of industrial society, almost everybody would become proletarian. The peasants would be drawn into the cities by economic necessity, and most of the bourgeoisie would become bankrupt by capitalist competition, and would sink into the proletariat. This has never happened; it was one of Marx's most famous wrong predictions. As industry advances the working classes grow, but the middle classes grow more rapidly still. There has never been a country in which the industrial workers were a majority. In most advanced countries, such as America, Great Britain, and Germany, the middle classes form a majority.

In the first chapter of *The Communist Manifesto,* Marx pictured Europe as being in the throes of a tremendous struggle for "the upper hand" between the rising bourgeoisie and the developing proletariat. The struggle was marked by strikes, lockouts, sabotage, wage slashes, bankruptcies, business crises, the simultaneous rise of industrial combines and trade unions, increasing proletarian "class consciousness" (realization of its nature and predicament), and violence. This vast dramatic clash between sharply contrasted antagonists was precisely the sort of thing a Romantic thinker would hope to find in society, especially a follower of Hegel, who believed that progress came about through "the fruitful struggle of opposite principles."

Following Hegel's Romantic tenets, Marx saw the contemporary struggle in Europe as only one chapter in the whole vast sweep of universal history, which they both believed to be a continuous evolutionary sequence of struggles between mutually interacting opposites, each struggle producing something higher that would in its turn struggle with its opposite. This supposed process of struggle and evolution, to which Hegel gave the celebrated name "dialectic," included absolutely everything, as Hegel presented it—God, spirit, reason, the universe, and man. Marx got rid of God, spirit, and some of the other abstractions, a process which he snidely called "standing Hegel on his head." This left him with an earthly, visible, tangible, material world as the scene of the evolutionary struggle—the subject mat-

ter of his celebrated doctrine, dialectical materialism. For Marx, the Romantic struggle of universal
history was reduced to an economic struggle between social classes. "The history of all hitherto
existing societies has been the history of class struggles."

In the first chapter of *The Communist Manifesto,*
Marx sketched the dramatic history of the world, the
struggles of ancient patricians and ancient slaves, of
feudal lords and feudal serfs, and above all, the
struggles of the bourgeoisie. For Marx, the bourgeoisie was the collective hero of a Romantic tragedy. Like many heroes of Romantic tragedies, the
bourgeoisie rose from low estate against enormous
odds, burst its chains and hurled the older masters
from their seats of power. Like many heroes of Romantic tragedies—Prometheus and Faust—the bourgeoisie was possessed of an enormous and restless
energy. Marx wrote, "It has accomplished wonders
far surpassing Egyptian pyramids, Roman aqueducts, Gothic cathedrals; it has conducted expeditions that have put in the shade all former migra-
tions of nations and crusades . . . it batters down
all Chinese walls." Finally, in Marx's view, the
bourgeoisie accomplished what so many Romantic
heroes strove for, what only God was previously
thought to have achieved: "In one word, it creates
a world in its own image."

Introduction

So far, Marx's bourgeoisie was the hero of a Romantic triumph beyond the dreams of Goethe or Byron. But this triumph was so Romantically extreme as to approach blasphemy. Nemesis, the goddess of retribution, lay in wait, as she did in so many other tragedies. In its pride of triumph the bourgeoisie became insolent, and in its insolence it forgot that in the depths from which it had risen so far, it was itself producing its fatal enemy, the proletariat. "What the bourgeoisie therefore produces, above all, are its own grave-diggers." The more the bourgeoisie produces, the stronger its subterranean antagonist grows. Marx believed that in the last act of this inevitable Romantic tragedy the bourgeoisie, grown old and tyrannical, would be hurled from its thrones into the abyss, like the haughty kings and insolent titans of so many Romantic dramas. "Its fall and the victory of the proletariat are equally inevitable."

In the full sense of the term, the first chapter of *The Communist Manifesto* is a high Romantic drama on a vast scale, in which the bourgeoisie plays the role of the most immense of all Romantic tragic heroes. It was doubtless very satisfying for Marx to feel that he understood and approved the course of the grand drama of history. One might ask why Marx threw himself so wholeheartedly into revolutionary work if he was convinced that the revolution would inevitably come at a given moment, no matter what he or the rest of the world did to hurry or prevent it. The answer, of course, is that Marx was possessed of an activist temperament, like many other believers in universal determinist schemes (e.g., Mohammed and Calvin). He was constantly driven from within to write, to make speeches, to organize, to act, driven by what the arch-Romantic Goethe would have called a *Daemon,* which meant not a devil, but an insatiable psychic compulsion. It is intellectually silly for a determinist to be an activist; all the efforts of Marx and his followers to make logic out of such illogic are unconvincing. Yet for Marx and his followers, these two inconsistent mental traits seemed to go naturally together.

The second chapter of *The Communist Manifesto,* "Proletarians and Communists," is essentially an argument with bourgeois critics of communism about whether communism is good or not. This was necessary at some point, for many things may be inevitable without being desirable (e.g., death and taxes). Marx began, "In what relation do the Communists stand to the proletarians as a whole?" The honest answer would have been that they stood in no relation to the proletarians, for there wasn't any communist organization to speak of. Instead, Marx wrote as if there was already a well organized international network of Communists which sought to offer its services to the various national proletarian movements, and to co-ordinate their revolutionary work.

The communist program was "the abolition of private property." This was expected to bring a thrill of horror to any bourgeois reader, and Marx spent the rest of the chapter arguing with and/or taunting such bourgeois readers. In this mock debate, Marx changed his tone drastically from the first chapter. He no longer sang of the bourgeoisie as heroes of a high historic drama; he squabbled with them and sneered at them as if the bourgeoisie were thieving, bloated, stupid villains of some vulgar horse opera—a tone that has been adopted by most people who call themselves Marxists.

Why should the bourgeoisie squawk about losing their private property, Marx wanted to know, when they themselves have stolen all their property from the hard-working, upstanding proletarians and farmers who produced it? Why should the bourgeoisie cry out that the Communists want to abolish freedom and individuality, when the bourgeoisie have themselves enslaved the huge majority of the population in the factories? The bourgeoisie moan that the Communists want to annihilate the state, culture, religion, and the family but they have themselves deprived the workers of any state, any culture, any true religion, and any decent family life, and so on.

This is certainly the least convincing part of *The Communist Manifesto*. The charges against the bourgeoisie are so exaggerated that one realizes that Marx was not entirely serious. He depicted the bourgeoisie screaming in chorus that the Communists wanted to nationalize all women, and then went on to assert that the bourgeoisie spent its own time seducing proletarian girls, and each other's wives as well. This, in the depths of the Victorian age, was presumably a heavy jest. Even if the arguments were true, all Marx proposed in this section was to drag the bourgeoisie down into the depths with the workers, apparently for the sake of sheer revenge. In other writings he dealt with the problem more seriously, and asserted that the abolition of bourgeois privilege would lead to a tremendous resurgence of true freedom, true creativity, and true culture among the former proletariat, which would more than make up for the loss of bourgeois freedom and culture in the revolution.

The chapter ends with Marx's famous ten-point communist program, which often startles and amuses modern readers by its combination of proposals that we still regard as "communist" or otherwise extremely radical—such as the nationalization of factories, banks, transport and land—with calls for reforms long established in advanced capitalist societies—such as income and inheritance taxes, and free public schools. The program was not intended to be a detailed or well-thought-out blueprint for the future beyond the revolution, nor was Marx ever to provide such a detailed blueprint in his other writings.

The last two chapters of *The Communist Manifesto* are only of historical interest, and not much of that. First Marx explained why he was right, and why every other group that called itself socialist was inadequate, unscientific, wrong, and vile. Right or wrong, all those groups soon disappeared as Marx predicted. Then Marx indicated his support—usually qualified—for various revolutionary groups scattered around Europe, the more extremist the better. None of those groups were destined to amount to anything. At the very end of the pamphlet, Marx returned to his vein of ringing Romantic rhetoric. He insisted on "the forcible overthrow of all existing social conditions" with uninhibited abandon. "Let the ruling classes tremble at a communist revolution. The proletarians have nothing to lose but their chains. They have a world to win. Working men of all countries, unite!" Millions have thrilled to this most memorable of all appeals that have come down to us from the Romantic age.

The Communist Manifesto had scarcely been published in February, 1848, when revolutions broke out in France and much of the rest of continental Europe, the climax of liberal political efforts in the Romantic age. Almost nothing happened as Marx had predicted. Everywhere the revolutionaries were bourgeois liberals and not socialist workingmen. Almost everywhere the primary revolutionary drive was toward national independence and unity. Everywhere the revolutions were put down in eighteen months or less. Only in France did some of the revolutionary events seem to confirm Marx's views. France was the only country in Europe that had secured national unity and independence and at the same time contained no significant national minorities within itself. Only in France, therefore, could the social struggle become more important than the national struggle.

The French revolution of February, 1848, was brought off by bourgeois liberals, like the other revolutions of the year. But in June there was actually a rising by some of the workers of Paris, which maintained itself behind the cobblestone barricades for a few days (the "June days" of socialist history) before being crushed in blood by the army. Marx was enthusiastic about this rising, for he thought it was the first genuine proletarian rebellion in history, the harbinger of a revolutionary future.

There were to be no more proletarian risings for over twenty years—rather frustrating years for

Marx. He lived mainly in London, and spent his time writing and organizing for the revolution. He developed his doctrines at great length in the book which Marxists think is his masterpiece, *Capital,* of which the first thousand-page-volume appeared in 1867. Here Marx's chief concern was to demonstrate the scientific foundations of his "scientific socialism." It is an encyclopedic work, one of the all-inclusive, high Romantic efforts to synthesize everything in a great field, like Darwin's *Origin of Species* and Wagner's cycle of operas, *The Niebelungen Ring.* Some of *Capital* is devoted to detailing Marx's philosophy, dialectical materialism. Most of it is devoted to economic and historical reasonings that were intended to prove Marx's theories about the bourgeoisie, the proletariat, and the revolution.

A man's convictions are more important than the reasons he later sets forth to justify them. Marx had already set forth his most important convictions in *The Communist Manifesto. Capital* has rarely convinced anyone who was not already bent toward Marxism. Economists, historians, and philosophers have long since ceased to take it as a serious contribution to their fields. It is so long and so dull a book that few Marxists can read or understand it. The function of *Capital* in the world of Marxist socialism is to sit on shelves, heavy and impressive, and to be pointed to as evidence that somewhere there is deep intellectual proof of what any given Marxist may happen to feel.

Most of Marx's organizational activities involved him in prolonged quarrels with other socialist leaders, notably the German trade unionist Ferdinand Lassalle and the Russian anarchist Mikhail Bakunin. He helped found an abortive workingmen's association in 1864, which is known in socialist history as The First International. His struggles to keep Bakunin from taking over the organization helped wreck it in the early 1870's. Marx was immensely enthused by the temporary success of the workers' rising in Paris after the French were defeated by the Prussians in the war of 1870-71. Some of the leaders of the rising, influenced by Marx's ideas, actually set up a "commune" to govern themselves, and seemed to foreshadow a socialist future.

Marx died in London in 1883, and his modest tomb in a dreary London cemetery has become a place of pilgrimage for thousands of Marxists from all over the world.

The great development of the organizations that profess Marxist doctrines came only after Marx's death. From the 1880's on, Marxist trade unions and Marxist political parties grew to major importance in most continental European countries, especially Germany, France, and Italy. As early as 1889 they formed an international co-ordinating committee, The Second International of socialist history. From the 1890's on, the bigger parties in the freer countries—notably Germany—began to moderate their bent toward violent revolution and extremism, and to evolve into reformist parties whose members were happy enough to live in capitalist societies. This was a long and often painful process, involving many accusations of heresy and many splits. It was finally completed only in the 1950's. Marxist socialists have ruled or helped rule almost every West European country, but there have been no successful workers' revolutions, and no proletarian states.

But the whole history of Marxist socialism was thrown into a completely new course by developments in Russia, a country whose revolutionary movement had interested Marx deeply, but certainly not a country in which an orthodox Marxist would have expected an early proletarian revolution. The reactionary tyranny of the Russian tsars, the worst in Europe, had provoked a revolutionary movement from the 1820's on, but the first Russian Marxist group was formed only in 1883, the year of Marx's death, by a few Russian revolutionaries exiled in Switzerland. It was Lenin, of course, who founded the important Russian Marxist party between 1900 and 1903—the Bolsheviki, who later renamed themselves "Communists" after Marx's term in *The Communist Manifesto*.

Introduction

But Lenin founded a very unorthodox Marxist party, if indeed it should be called Marxist at all. Lenin learned to be an atheist, a revolutionary, and a socialist from other native Russian revolutionaries, not from Marx. He picked up the doctrine of dialectical materialism from the Russian revolutionary N. G. Chernyshevskii, not from Marx. He formed his plans for the Bolshevik party, a tiny, well-disciplined, conspiratorial, elite group in a vast backward peasant country, from earlier Russian revolutionary theory and practice, not from Marx, who had rejected such ideas as "unscientific adventurism." Lenin absorbed his faith that Russia could be the first country to revolt, establish socialism, and save the world, by reading other Russian revolutionaries, and not from Marx who could never swallow such "Russian messianic" ideas. Of all the theories that Lenin combined in his Bolshevik program, the only specially Marxist ideas of importance were (1) the "scientific" notion of the inevitability of a socialist revolution, and (2) the emphasis on the proletariat.

In practice, Lenin's Bolshevikis were even less Marxist than this. Lenin made his proletarian revolution in Russia in 1917, when the proletariat formed less than ten per cent of the Russian population. Lenin won more with the help of peasant soldiers than of workers. In short, he carried through a revolution in conditions that Marx would have denounced as impossible, and in a manner that most of the orthodox Marxists of Russia and Europe denounced as un-Marxist.

Nevertheless, Lenin and all Communists ever since have had the unshakable conviction that they alone are the true Marxists. They go through all the motions of studying and revering Marx's works, especially *The Communist Manifesto.* Since there are thirteen or fourteen communist states and no other Marxist governments, and since there are millions more Communists than any other kind of Marxist in the world, it becomes somewhat perverse and sectarian to deny the Communists the label "Marxist" that they so passionately claim. Perhaps Stalin, who killed workers in Russia, has as good a claim to be called "Marxist" as a Western Marxist socialist such as former Prime Minister Guy Mollet of France, who killed workers in Algeria.

Certainly Marx's chief claim to historical importance is the use the Communists have put him to. Marx was not himself a very attractive man. His great intellectual synthesis of many strains of thought current in his high Romantic age strikes most of us as obsolete, a huge monument from a vanished era. His youthful work, *The Communist Manifesto,* has had a tremendous effect. It denounces the injustices of the early industrial revolution not wisely but too well. It urges bloody violence as a means for reaching a free and equal society. It divides men into irreconcilably hostile classes, and glorifies the struggle between them, in hope that the result will be for the good. All these thoughts and sentiments flourished in Marx's day, and their inclusion by Marx in *The Communist Manifesto* is one of the most important and ambivalent legacies to come down to us from the Romantic age.

Francis B. Randall

Selected Bibliography

*Barzun, J. *Darwin, Marx, Wagner: Critique of a Heritage*. pap. New York: Doubleday, 1958.

————. *Romanticism and the Modern Ego*. Boston: Little, Brown, 1943.

*Berlin, I. *Karl Marx: His Life and Environment*. pap. Oxford: Oxford University Press, 1948.

Bernstein, E. *Evolutionary Socialism*. Translated by Edith C. Harvey. pap. New York: Schocken, 1961.

Carr, E. H. *A History of Soviet Russia*. 6 vols. New York: Macmillan, 1952-59.

Chamberlin, W. H. *The Russian Revolution, 1917-1921*. 2 vols. New York: Macmillan, 1935.

Clarkson, J. *A History of Russia*. New York: Random, 1961.

*Cole, G. D. H. *Socialist Thought*. 5 vols. New York: St Martins, 1953-60.

Deutscher, I. *Stalin: A Political Biography*. pap. New York: Vintage, 1960.

Selected Bibliography

Dill, M. *Germany: A Modern History.* Ann Arbor: University of Michigan, 1961.

Eastman, M. *Marxism: Is It Science?* New York: W. W. Norton, 1940.

Engels, F. *Anti-Dühring.* Translated by Emile Burns, edited by C. P. Dutt. New York: International Publishers, 1935.

Gurian, W. *Rise and Decline of Marxism.* Translated by E. F. Peeler. London: Burns, Oates and Washbourne, 1958.

Haimson, L. *The Russian Marxists and the Origins of Bolshevism.* Cambridge: Harvard University, 1955.

*Heilbroner, R. *The Worldly Philosophers.* New York: Simon & Schuster, 1961.

Hillquit, M. *From Marx to Lenin.* New York: Hanford, 1921.

*Hook, S. *From Hegel to Marx.* New York: Humanities, 1950.

———. *The Hero in History.* New York: Humanities, 1960.

Hunt, R. N. Carew. *Marxism: Past and Present.* New York: Macmillan, 1955.

*———. *The Theory and Practice of Communism.* New York: Macmillan, 1957.

Kautsky, K. *Ethics and Materialistic Conception of History.* Translated by John B. Askew. Chicago: C. H. Kerr, 1907.

————. *Social Democracy versus Communism.* Edited and translated by David Shub and Joseph Shaplen. New York: The Rand School Press, 1946.

Kohn, H. *The Mind of Germany.* New York: Scribner, 1960.

Lenin, V. *Selected Works.* 12 vols. New York: International Publishers, 1935-38.

Marx, K. *Capital.* Translated by Samuel Moore and Edward Aveling. Vol. I. London: ————, 1887. Vols. II and III. Chicago: C. H. Kerr, c. 1909-12.

————. *The Class Struggles in France, 1848-1850.* New York: International Publishers, 1934.

————. *Marx vs. Russia.* Edited by J. A. Doerig. New York: Unger, 1962.

Mehnert, K. *Stalin vs. Marx.* New York: Macmillan, 1952.

*Mehring, F. *Karl Marx: The Story of His Life.* pap. New York: Putnam, 1963.

Mitrany, D. *Marx Against the Peasant.* pap. New York: Collier, 1961.

Nomad, M. *Apostles of Revolution.* pap. New York: Collier, 1961.

Pinson, K. *Modern Germany.* New York: Macmillan, 1954.

Plamenatz, J. *German Marxism and Russian Communism.* New York: Longmans, 1954.

*Popper, K. *The Open Society and Its Enemies.* Princeton: Princeton University, 1950.

Randall, J. H., Jr. *The Making of the Modern Mind.* Boston: Houghton Mifflin, 1940.

Schapiro, L. *The Communist Party of the Soviet Union.* New York: Random, 1959.

*Schumpeter, J. *Capitalism, Socialism and Democracy.* New York: Harper, 1950.

Shub, D. *Lenin.* New York: New American Library, 1951.

Simkhovitch, V. *Marxism Versus Socialism.* Boston: Ginn, 1908.

Souvarine, B. *Stalin.* New York: Longmans Green, 1939.

Stalin, J. *Problems of Leninism.* New York: International Publishers, 1934.

Treadgold, D. *Twentieth Century Russia.* New York: Rand McNally, 1959.

Trotsky, L. *History of the Russian Revolution.* Translated by Max Eastman. Ann Arbor: University of Michigan, 1957.

*Wilson, E. *To the Finland Station.* pap. New York: Doubleday, 1953.

Wolf, B. *Three Who Made a Revolution.* New York: Dial, 1960.

---

* These books are of special value for information and understanding of Karl Marx and his work.

Preface to the English Edition[1] of 1888

THE *Manifesto* was published as the platform of the Communist League, a workingmen's association, first exclusively German, later on international, and, under the political conditions of the Continent before 1848, unavoidably a secret society. At a congress of the League, held in London in November, 1847, Marx and Engels were commissioned to prepare for publication a complete theoretical and practical party program. Drawn up in German, in January, 1848, the manuscript was sent to the printer in London a few weeks before the French revolution of February 24th. A French translation was brought out in Paris, shortly before the insurrection of June, 1848. The first English translation, by Miss Helen Macfarlane, appeared in George Julian Harney's *Red Republican,* London,

---

[1] This is Engels' best Preface. Several of the lesser Prefaces to other editions are to be found in the Addenda of this edition.—*Ed.*

1850. A Danish and a Polish edition had also been published.

The defeat of the Parisian insurrection of June, 1848—the first great battle between proletariat and bourgeoisie—drove again into the background, for a time, the social and political aspirations of the European working class. Thenceforth, the struggle for supremacy was again, as it had been before the revolution of February, solely between different sections of the propertied class; the working class was reduced to a fight for political elbowroom and to the position of extreme wing of the middle-class radicals. Wherever independent proletarian movements continued to show signs of life, they were ruthlessly hunted down. Thus the Prussian police hunted out the Central Board of the Communist League, then located in Cologne. The members were arrested, and, after eighteen months' imprisonment, they were tried in October, 1852. This celebrated "Cologne Communist trial" lasted from October 4th till November 12th; seven of the prisoners were sentenced to terms of imprisonment in a fortress, varying from three to six years. Immediately after the sentence, the League was formally dissolved by the remaining members. As to the *Manifesto,* it seemed thenceforth to be doomed to oblivion.

When the European working class had recovered

sufficient strength for another attack on the ruling classes, the International Workingmen's Association sprang up. But this association, formed with the express aim of welding into one body the whole militant proletariat of Europe and America, could not at once proclaim the principles laid down in the *Manifesto*. The International was bound to have a program broad enough to be acceptable to the English trades' unions, to the followers of Proudhon in France, Belgium, Italy, and Spain, and to the Lassalleans[2] in Germany. Marx, who drew up this program to the satisfaction of all parties, entirely trusted to the intellectual development of the working class, which was sure to result from combined action and mutual discussion. The very events and vicissitudes of the struggle against capital, the defeats even more than the victories, could not help bringing home to men's minds the insufficiency of their various favorite nostrums, and preparing the way for a more complete insight into the true conditions of working-class emancipation. And Marx was right. The International, on its breaking up in 1874, left the workers quite different men from what it had found them in 1864. Proudhonism in France,

---

[2] Lassalle personally, to us, always acknowledged himself to be a disciple of Marx, and, as such, stood on the ground of the *Manifesto*. But in his public agitation, 1862-64, he did not go beyond demanding co-operative workshops supported by state credit. [*Note by Engels.*]

Lassalleanism in Germany were dying out, and even the conservative English trades' unions, though most of them had long since severed their connection with the International, were gradually advancing toward that point at which, last year at Swansea, their president could say in their name, "Continental Socialism has lost its terrors for us." In fact, the principles of the *Manifesto* had made considerable headway among the workingmen of all countries.

The *Manifesto* itself thus came to the front again. The German text had been, since 1850, reprinted several times in Switzerland, England and America. In 1872, it was translated into English in New York, where the translation was published in *Woodhull and Claflin's Weekly*. From this English version, a French one was made in *Le Socialiste* of New York. Since then at least two more English translations, more or less mutilated, have been brought out in America, and one of them has been reprinted in England. The first Russian translation, made by Bakunin, was published at Herzen's *Kolokol* office in Geneva, about 1863; a second one, by the heroic Vera Zasulich,[3] also in Geneva, 1882. A new Danish edition is to be found in *Social-*

---

[3] Later on Engels himself rightly pointed out in the afterword to the article "Social Relations in Russia," published in *Internationales aus dem Volksstaat (1871-75)*, Berlin, 1894, that the actual translator was G. V. Plekhanov.—*Ed.*

demokratisk Bibliothek, Copenhagen, 1885; a fresh French translation in *Le Socialiste,* Paris, 1885. From this latter a Spanish version was prepared and published in Madrid, 1886. The German reprints are not to be counted—there have been at least twelve. An Armenian translation, which was to be published in Constantinople some months ago, did not see the light, I am told, because the publisher was afraid of bringing out a book with the name of Marx on it, while the translator declined to call it his own production. Of further translations into other languages I have heard, but have not seen them. Thus the history of the *Manifesto* reflects, to a great extent, the history of the modern working-class movement; at present it is undoubtedly the most widespread, the most international production of all socialist literature, the common platform acknowledged by millions of workingmen from Siberia to California.

Yet, when it was written, we could not have called it a *socialist* manifesto. By Socialists, in 1847, were understood, on the one hand, the adherents of the various Utopian systems: Owenites in England, Fourierists in France, both of them already reduced to the position of mere sects gradually dying out; on the other hand, the most multifarious social quacks, who, by all manners of tinkering, professed to redress, without any danger to capital and profit, all sorts of social grievances, in both cases men outside the working-class movement, and looking rather to the "educated" classes for support. Whatever portion of the working class had become convinced of the insufficiency of mere political revolutions and had proclaimed the necessity of a total social change, that portion then called itself communist. It was a crude, rough-hewn, purely instinctive sort of communism; still, it touched the cardinal point and was powerful enough amongst the working class to produce the Utopian communism, in France, of Cabet, and in Germany, of Weitling. Thus, socialism was, in 1847, a middle-class movement; communism, a working-class movement. Socialism was, on the Continent at least, "respectable"; Communism was the very opposite. And as our notion, from the very beginning, was that "the emancipation of the working class must be the act of the working class itself," there could be no doubt as to which of the two names we must take. Moreover, we have, ever since, been far from repudiating it.

The *Manifesto* being our joint production, I consider myself bound to state that the fundamental proposition, which forms its nucleus, belongs to Marx. That proposition is: that in every historical epoch, the prevailing mode of economic production and exchange, and the social organization necessarily following from it, form the basis upon which is built up, and from which alone can be explained, the political and intellectual history of that epoch; that consequently the whole history of mankind (since the dissolution of primitive tribal society, holding land in common ownership) has been a history of class struggles, contests between exploiting and exploited, ruling and oppressed classes; that the history of these class struggles forms a series of evolutions in which, nowadays, a stage has been reached where the exploited and oppressed class—the proletariat—cannot attain its emancipation from the sway of the exploiting and ruling class—the bourgeoisie—without, at the same time, and once and for all, emancipating society at large from all exploitation, oppression, class distinctions, and class struggles.

This proposition that, in my opinion, is destined to do for history what Darwin's theory has done for biology, we, both of us, had been gradually approaching for some years before 1845. How far I had independently progressed toward it, is best shown by my *Condition of the Working Class in England*.[4] But when I again met Marx in Brussels,

---

[4] *The Condition of the Working Class in England in 1844.* By Friedrich Engels. Translated by Florence K. Wischnewetzky, New York: Lovell—London: W. Reeves, 1888. [*Note by Engels.*]

in spring, 1845, he had it already worked out, and put it before me, in terms almost as clear as those in which I have stated it here.

From our joint preface to the German edition of 1872, I quote the following:

However much the state of things may have altered during the last twenty-five years, the general principles laid down in this *Manifesto* are, on the whole, as correct today as ever. Here and there some detail might be improved. The practical application of the principles will depend, as the *Manifesto* itself states, everywhere and at all times, on the historical conditions existing at the time, and, for that reason, no special stress is laid on the revolutionary measures proposed at the end of Section II. That passage would, in many respects, be very differently worded today. In view of the gigantic strides of modern industry since 1848, and of the accompanying improved and extended organization of the working class, in view of the practical experience gained, first in the February revolution, and then, still more, in the Paris Commune, where the proletariat for the first time held political power for two whole months, this program has in some details become antiquated. One thing especially was proved by the Commune, *viz.*, that "the working class cannot simply lay hold of the ready-made state machinery and wield it for its own purposes." (See *The Civil War in France*; *Address of the General Council of the International Working Men's Association,* London: Truelove, 1871, p. 15,[5] where this point is further developed.) Further, it is self-evident, that the criticism of socialist literature is deficient in relation to the present time, because it comes down only to 1847; also, that the remarks on the relation of the Communists to the various opposition parties (Section IV), although in principle still correct, yet in practice are antiquated, because the political situation has been entirely changed, and the progress of history has swept from off the earth the greater portion of the political parties there enumerated.

But then, the *Manifesto* has become a historical document which we have no longer any right to alter.

The present translation is by Mr. Samuel Moore, the translator of the greater portion of Marx's *Capital.* We have revised it in common,

---

[5] K. Marx and F. Engels, *Selected Works,* 2 vols., Vol. I, Moscow, 1951, p. 468 ff.—*Ed.*

Preface

and I have added a few notes explanatory of historical allusions.

Friedrich Engels

London, 30th January, 1888

The Communist Manifesto

A SPECTER is haunting Europe—the specter of communism. All the powers of old Europe have entered into a holy alliance to hunt down and exorcise this specter: Pope and Tsar, Metternich and Guizot, French Radicals and German police-spies.

Where is the party in opposition that has not been denounced as communistic by its opponents in power? Where the opposition that has not hurled back the branding reproach of communism against the more advanced opposition parties, as well as against its reactionary adversaries?

Two things result from this fact:

I. Communism is already acknowledged by all European powers to be itself a *power*.

II. It is high time that Communists should openly, in the face of the whole world, publish their views, their aims, their tendencies, and meet this nursery tale of the *specter of communism* with a manifesto of the party itself.

To this end, Communists of various nationalities have assembled in London and sketched the following *Manifesto*, to be published in the English, French, German, Italian, Flemish, and Danish languages.

I

Bourgeois
and Proletarians[1]

THE history of all hitherto existing society[2] is the history of class struggles.

---

[1] By bourgeois is meant the people in the class of modern capitalists, owners of the means of social production and employers of wage labor. By proletarians, the people in the class of modern wage laborers who, having no means of production of their own, are reduced to selling their labor power in order to live.

[2] That is, all *written* history. In 1847, the prehistory of society, the social organization existing previous to recorded history, was all but unknown. Since then, Haxthausen discovered common ownership of land in Russia, Maurer proved it to be the social foundation from which all Teutonic races started in history, and by and by village communities were found to be, or to have been the primitive form of society everywhere from India to Ireland. The inner organization of this primitive communistic society was laid bare, in its typical form, by Morgan's crowning discovery of the true nature of the *gens* and its relation to the *tribe*. With the dissolution of these primeval communities society begins to be differentiated into separate and finally antagonistic classes. I have attempted to retrace this process of dissolution in: *Der Ursprung der Familie, des Privateigenthums und des Staats*. [*The Origin of the Family, Private Property, and the State*], 2nd edition, Stuttgart, 1886. [*Note by Engels in the edition of 1888.*]

The Communist Manifesto

Freeman and slave, patrician and plebeian, lord and serf, guildmaster[3] and journeyman, in a word, oppressor and oppressed, stood in constant opposition to one another, carried on an uninterrupted, now hidden, now open fight, a fight that each time ended, either in a revolutionary reconstitution of society at large, or in the common ruin of the struggling classes.

In the earlier epochs of history, we find almost everywhere a complicated arrangement of society into various orders, a manifold gradation of social rank. In ancient Rome we have patricians, knights, plebeians, slaves; in the Middle Ages, feudal lords, vassals, guildmasters, journeymen, apprentices, serfs; and in almost all of these particular classes, again, other subordinate gradations.

The modern bourgeois society that has sprouted from the ruins of feudal society has not done away with class antagonisms. It has only established new classes, new conditions of oppression, new forms of struggle in place of the old ones.

Our epoch, the epoch of the bourgeoisie, shows, however, this distinctive feature: it has simplified the class antagonisms. Society as a whole is more and more splitting up into two great hostile camps,

[3] Guildmaster, that is, a full member of a guild, a master within, not a head of a guild. [*Note by Engels in the edition of 1888.*]

into two great classes directly facing each other: *bourgeoisie* and *proletariat.*

From the serfs of the Middle Ages sprang the chartered burghers of the earliest towns. From these burghers the first elements of the bourgeoisie were developed.

The discovery of America, the rounding of the Cape, opened up fresh ground for the rising bourgeoisie. The East-Indian and Chinese markets, the colonization of America, trade with the colonies, the increase in the means of exchange and in commodities generally, gave to commerce, to navigation, to industry, an impulse never before known, and thereby, to the revolutionary element in the tottering feudal society, a rapid development.

The feudal system of industry, under which industrial production was monopolized by closed guilds, now no longer sufficed for the growing wants of the new markets. The manufacturing system took its place. The guildmasters were pushed on one side by the manufacturing middle class; division of labor between the different corporate guilds vanished in the face of division of labor in each single workshop.

Meanwhile the markets kept on growing; demand went on rising. Manufacturing no longer was able to keep up with this growth. Then, steam and machinery revolutionized industrial production. The place of manufacture was taken by the giant, *modern industry*; the place of the industrial middle class, by industrial millionaires, the leaders of whole industrial armies, the modern bourgeois.

Modern industry has established the world market, for which the discovery of America paved the way. This market has given an immense development to commerce, to navigation, to communication by land. This development has, in its turn, reacted on the extension of industry; and in proportion as industry, commerce, navigation, railways extended, in the same proportion the bourgeoisie developed, increased its capital, and pushed into the background every class handed down from the Middle Ages.

We see, therefore, how the modern bourgeosie is itself the product of a long course of development, of a series of revolutions in the modes of production and of exchange.

Each step in the development of the bourgeoisie was accompanied by a corresponding political advance of that class. An oppressed class under the sway of the feudal nobility, an armed and self-governing association in the medieval commune:[4]

---

[4] "Commune" was the name taken, in France, by the nascent towns even before they had wrested from their feudal lords and masters local self-government and political rights as the "Third Estate." Generally speaking, for the economical development of the bourgeoisie, England

here an independent urban republic (as in Italy and
Germany); there taxable "third estate" of the monarchy (as in France); afterward, in the period of
manufacturing proper, serving either the semi-feudal
or the absolute monarchy as a counterpoise against
the nobility, and, in fact, a cornerstone of the great
monarchies in general, the bourgeoisie has at last,
since the establishment of modern industry and of
the world market, conquered for itself, in the modern representative state, exclusive political sway.
The executive of the modern state is but a committee
for managing the common affairs of the whole
bourgeoisie.

The bourgeoisie, historically, has played a most
revolutionary part.

The bourgeoisie, wherever it has got the upper
hand, has put an end to all feudal, patriarchal, idyllic
relations. It has pitilessly torn asunder the motley
feudal ties that bound man to his "natural super-
iors," and has left remaining no other bond between
man and man than naked self-interest and callous
"cash payment." It has drowned the most heavenly

---

is here taken as the typical country; for its political development, France. [*Note by Engels in the edition of 1888.*]

This was the name given their urban communities by
the townsmen of Italy and France, after they had pur-
chased or wrested their initial rights of self-government
from their feudal lords. [*Note by Engels in the edition of
1890.*]

ecstasies of religious fervor, of chivalrous enthusiasm, of philistine sentimentalism, in the icy water of egotistical calculation. It has resolved personal worth into exchange value, and in place of the numberless indefeasible chartered freedoms, has set up that single, unconscionable freedom—free trade. In one word, for exploitation, veiled by religious and political illusions, it has substituted naked, shameless, direct, brutal exploitation.

The bourgeoisie has stripped of its halo every occupation hitherto honored and looked up to with reverent awe. It has converted the physician, the lawyer, the priest, the poet, the man of science, into its paid wage laborers.

The bourgeoisie has torn away from the family its sentimental veil, and has reduced the family relation to a mere money relation.

The bourgeoisie has disclosed how it came to pass that the brutal display of vigor in the Middle Ages, which reactionaries so much admire, found its fitting complement in the laziest indolence. It has been the first to show what man's activity can bring about. It has accomplished wonders far surpassing Egyptian pyramids, Roman aqueducts, and Gothic cathedrals; it has conducted expeditions that put to shame all former Exoduses of nations and crusades.

The bourgeoisie cannot exist without constantly revolutionizing the instruments of production, and thereby the relations of production, and with them the whole relations of society. Conservation of the old modes of production in unaltered form, was, on the contrary, the first condition of existence for all earlier industrial classes. Constant revolutionizing of production, uninterrupted disturbance of all social conditions, everlasting uncertainty and agitation distinguish the bourgeois epoch from all earlier ones. All fixed, fast-frozen relations, with their train of ancient and venerable prejudices and opinions are swept away, all new-formed ones become antiquated before they can ossify. All that is solid melts into air, all that is holy is profaned, and man is at last compelled to face his real conditions of life, and his mutual relations with sober eye.

The need of a constantly expanding market for its products chases the bourgeoisie over the whole surface of the globe. It must nestle everywhere, settle everywhere, establish connections everywhere.

The bourgeoisie has through its exploitation of the world market given a cosmopolitan character to production and consumption in every country. To the great chagrin of reactionaries, it has drawn from under the feet of industry the national ground on which it stood. All old-established national industries have been destroyed or are daily being destroyed. They are dislodged by new industries, whose introduction becomes a life and death question for all civilized nations, by industries that no longer work up indigenous raw material, but raw material drawn from the remotest zones; industries whose products are consumed, not only at home, but in every quarter of the globe. In place of the old wants, satisfied by the productions of the country, we find new wants, requiring for their satisfaction the products of distant lands and climates. In place of the old local and national seclusion and self-sufficiency, we have intercourse in every direction, universal inter-dependence of nations. And as in material, so also in intellectual production. The intellectual creations of individual nations become common property. National one-sidedness and nar-row-mindedness become more and more impossible, and from the numerous national and local literatures, there emerges a world literature.

The bourgeoisie, by the rapid improvement of all instruments of production, by the immensely facili-tated means of communication, draws all, even the most backward, nations into civilization. The cheap prices of its commodities are the heavy artillery with which it batters down all Chinese walls, with which it forces the underdeveloped nations' intensely ob-stinate hatred of foreigners to capitulate. It compels all nations, on pain of extinction, to adopt the bour-geois mode of production; it compels them to in-troduce what it calls civilization into their midst, *i.e.*, to become bourgeois themselves. In one word, it creates a world in its own image.

The bourgeoisie has subjected rural areas to the rule of cities. It has created enormous cities, has greatly increased the urban population as compared with the rural, and has thus rescued a considerable part of the population from the idiocy of rural life. Just as it has made the country dependent on the cities, so has it made barbarian and semi-under-developed countries dependent on the civilized ones, nations of peasants on nations of bourgeois, the East on the West.

The bourgeoisie keeps more and more doing away with the scattered state of the population, of the means of production, and of property. It has agglomerated population, centralized means of production, and has concentrated property in a few hands. The necessary consequence of this was political centralization. Independent, or but loosely connected, provinces with separate interests, laws, governments, and systems of taxation became lumped together into one nation, with one govern-ment, one code of laws, one national class-interest, one frontier, and one customs-tariff.

The bourgeoisie, during its rule of scarcely one hundred years, has created more massive and more colossal productive forces than have all preceding generations together. Subjection of Nature's forces to man, machinery, application of chemistry to industry and agriculture, steam-navigation, railways, electric telegraphs, clearing of whole continents for cultivation, canalization of rivers, whole populations conjured out of the ground—what earlier century had even a presentiment that such productive forces slumbered in the lap of social labor?

We see then: the means of production and of exchange, on whose foundation the bourgeoisie built itself up, were generated in feudal society. At a certain stage in the development of these means of production and of exchange, the conditions under which feudal society produced and exchanged, the feudal organization of agriculture and manufacturing industry, in one word, the feudal relations of property became no longer compatible with the already developed productive forces; they became so many fetters. They had to be burst asunder; they were burst asunder.

Into their place stepped free competition, accompanied by a social and political constitution adapted to it, and by the economical and political sway of the bourgeois class.

A similar movement is going on before our own eyes. Modern bourgeois society with its relations of production, of exchange and of property, a society that has conjured up such gigantic means of production and of exchange, is like the sorcerer, who is

66

no longer able to control the powers of the subterranean world which he has called up by his spells. For many decades now the history of industry and commerce has been but the history of the revolt of modern productive forces against modern conditions of production, against the property relations that are the conditions for the existence of the bourgeoisie and of its rule. It is enough to mention the commercial crises that by their periodical return put on trial, each time more threateningly, the existence of the entire bourgeois society. In these crises a great part not only of the existing products, but also of the previously created productive forces, are periodically destroyed. In these crises there breaks out an epidemic that, in all earlier epochs, would have seemed an absurdity—the epidemic of over-production. Society suddenly finds itself put back into a state of momentary barbarism; it appears as if a famine, a universal war of devastation had cut off the supply of every means of subsistence; industry and commerce seem to be destroyed; and why? Because there is too much civilization, too much means of subsistence, too much industry, too much commerce. The productive forces at the disposal of society no longer tend to further the development of the conditions of bourgeois property; on the contrary, they have become too powerful for these conditions, by which they are fettered, and so soon as they overcome these fetters, they bring disorder into the whole of bourgeois society, endanger the existence of bourgeois property. The conditions of bourgeois society are too narrow to comprise the wealth created by them. And how does the bourgeoisie get over these crises? On the one hand by enforced destruction of a mass of productive forces; on the other, by the conquest of new markets, and by the more thorough exploitation of the old ones. That is to say, by paving the way for more extensive and more destructive crises, and by diminishing the means whereby crises are prevented.

The weapons with which the bourgeoisie felled feudalism to the ground are now turned against the bourgeoisie itself.

But not only has the bourgeoisie forged the weapons that bring death to itself; it has also called into existence the men who are to wield those weapons—the modern working class—the proletarians.

In proportion as the bourgeoisie, *i.e.*, capital, is developed, in the same proportion is the proletariat, the modern working class, developed—a class of laborers, who live only so long as they find work, and who find work only so long as their labor increases capital. These laborers, who must sell themselves piecemeal, are a commodity, like every other article of commerce, and are consequently exposed to all the vicissitudes of competition, to all the fluctuations of the market.

Owing to the extensive use of machinery and to division of labor, the work of the proletarians has lost all individual character, and, consequently, all charm for the workman. He becomes an appendage of the machine, and it is only the most simple, most monotonous, and most easily acquired knack that is required of him. Hence, the cost of production of a workman is restricted, almost entirely, to the means of subsistence that he requires for his maintenance, and for the propagation of his race. But the price of a commodity, and therefore also of labor,[5] is equal to its cost of production. In proportion, therefore, as the repulsiveness of the work increases, the wage decreases. What is more, in proportion as the use of machinery and division of labor increases, in the same proportion the burden of toil also increases, whether by prolongation of the working hours, by increase of the work exacted in a given time or by increased speed of the machinery, etc.

Modern industry has converted the little workshop of the patriarchal master into the great factory

---

[5] Subsequently Marx pointed out that the worker does not sell his labor but his labor power. See in this connection Engels' introduction to Marx's *Wage Labor and Capital*, 1891, in K. Marx and F. Engels, *Selected Works*, Eng. ed., Vol. I, Moscow, 1951, pp. 66-73.—*Ed.*

of the industrial capitalist. Masses of laborers, crowded into the factory, are organized like soldiers. As privates of the industrial army they are placed under the command of a perfect hierarchy of officers and sergeants. Not only are they slaves of the bourgeois class, and of the bourgeois state; they are daily and hourly enslaved by the machine, by the foreman, and, above all, by the individual bourgeois manufacturer himself. The more openly this despotism proclaims gain to be its end and aim, the more petty, the more hateful, and the more embittering it is.

The less the skill and exertion of strength implied in manual labor, in other words, the more modern industry becomes developed, the more is the labor of men superseded by that of women. Differences in age and sex have no longer any distinctive social validity for the working class. All are instruments of labor, more or less expensive to use, according to their age and sex.

No sooner is the exploitation of the laborer by the manufacturer, so far, at an end, that he receives his wages in cash, than he is set upon by the other portions of the bourgeoisie, the landlord, the shopkeeper, the pawnbroker, etc.

The lower strata of the middle class—the small tradespeople, shopkeepers, and retired tradesmen generally, the handicraftsmen, and farmers—all these sink gradually into the proletariat, partly because their diminutive capital does not suffice for the scale on which modern industry is carried on, and is swamped in the competition with large capitalists, partly because their specialized skill is rendered worthless by new methods of production. Thus the proletariat is recruited from all classes of the population.

The proletariat goes through various stages of development. With its birth begins its struggle with the bourgeoisie. At first the contest is carried on by individual laboreres, then by the workers of a factory, then by the members of one trade, in one locality, against the individual bourgeois who directly exploits them. They direct their attacks not against the bourgeois conditions of production, but against the instruments of production themselves; they destroy imported wares that compete with their labor, they smash machinery to pieces, they set factories ablaze, they seek to restore by force the vanished status of the workman of the Middle Ages.

At this stage the laborers still form an incoherent mass scattered over the whole country, and broken up by their mutual competition. If the workers unite at all this is not yet the consequence of their own initiative, but of the union of the bourgeoisie, which class, in order to attain its own political ends, is compelled to set the whole proletariat in motion, and is moreover still able to do so. At this stage, therefore, the proletarians do not fight their enemies, but the enemies of their enemies, the remnants of absolute monarchy, the landowners, the nonindustrial bourgeoisie, the petty bourgeoisie. Thus the whole historical movement is concentrated in the hands of the bourgeoisie; every victory so obtained is a victory for the bourgeoisie.

But with the development of industry the proletariat not only increases in number; it becomes concentrated in greater masses, its strength grows, and it feels that strength more. The various interests and conditions of life within the ranks of the proletariat are more and more equalized, in proportion as machinery obliterates all distinctions of labor, and nearly everywhere reduces wages to the same low level. The growing competition among the bourgeoisie, and the resulting commercial crises, make the wages of the workers ever more fluctuating. The unceasing improvement of machinery, ever more rapidly developing, makes their livelihood more and more precarious; the collisions between individual workmen and individual bourgeoisie take more and more the character of collisions between two classes. Thereupon the workers begin to form combinations (trade unions) against the bourgeoisie; they club together in order to keep up the rate of wages; they found permanent associations in order to make provision beforehand for these occasional revolts. Here and there the contest breaks out into riots.

From time to time the workers are victorious, but only for a time. The real fruit of their battles lies not in the immediate result, but in the ever-expanding union of the workers. This union is helped by the improved means of communication that are created by modern industry and that place the workers of different localities in contact with one another. It was just this contact that was needed to centralize the numerous local struggles, all of the same character, into one national struggle between classes. But every class struggle is a political struggle. And that union, to attain which the burghers of the Middle Ages, with their miserable highways, required centuries, the modern proletarians, thanks to railways, achieve in a few years.

This organization of the proletarians into a class, and consequently into a political party, is continually being upset again by the competition among the workers themselves. But it constantly rises up again, stronger, firmer, mightier. It compels legislative recognition of particular interests of the workers, by taking advantage of the divisions among the bourgeoisie itself. Thus was the ten-hours' bill in England carried.

Moreover, collisions between the classes of the

old society advance, in many ways, the course of development of the proletariat. The bourgeoisie finds itself involved in a constant battle. At first with the aristocracy; later on, with those portions of the bourgeoisie itself, whose interests have become antagonistic to the progress of industry; at all times, with the bourgeoisie of foreign countries. In all these battles it sees itself compelled to appeal to the proletariat, to ask for its help, and thus, to drag it into the political arena. The bourgeoisie itself, therefore, supplies the proletariat with its own elements of political and general education, in other words, it furnishes the proletariat with weapons for fighting the bourgeoisie.

Further, as we have already seen, entire sections of the ruling classes are, by the advance of industry, precipitated into the proletariat, or are at least threatened in their conditions of existence. These also supply the proletariat with fresh elements of enlightenment and progress.

Finally, in times when the class struggle nears the decisive hour, the process of dissolution going on within the ruling class, in fact within the whole range of old society, assumes such a violent, glaring character, that a small section of the ruling class cuts itself adrift, and joins the revolutionary class, the class that holds the future in its hands. Just as, therefore, at an earlier period, a section of the nobility went over to the bourgeoisie, so now a portion of the bourgeoisie goes over to the proletariat, and in particular, a portion of the bourgeois ideologists, who have raised themselves to the level of comprehending theoretically the historical movement as a whole.

Of all the classes that stand face to face with the bourgeoisie today, the proletariat alone is a really revolutionary class. The other classes decay and finally disappear in the face of modern industry; the proletariat is its special and essential product.

The lower middle class, the small manufacturer, the shopkeeper, the artisan, the peasant, all these fight against the bourgeoisie, to save from extinction their existence as fractions of the middle class. They are therefore not revolutionary, but conservative. What is more, they are reactionary, for they try to roll back the wheel of history. If by chance they are revolutionary, they are so only in view of their impending transfer into the proletariat, they thus defend not their present, but their future interests, they desert their own standpoint to place themselves at that of the proletariat.

The "dangerous class,"[6] the social scum, that passively rotting mass thrown off by the lowest layers of old society, may, here and there, be swept into

----

[6] The "Lumpenproletariat" in German.—*Ed.*

the movement by a proletarian revolution; its conditions of life, however, prepare it far more for the part of a bribed tool of reactionary intrigue.

The living conditions of the old society at large are already virtually swamped by the living conditions of the proletariat. The proletarian is without property; his relation to his wife and children has no longer anything in common with the bourgeois family relations; modern industrial labor, modern subjection to capital, the same in England as in France, in America as in Germany, has stripped him of every trace of national character. Law, morality, religion, are to him so many bourgeois prejudices, behind which lurk in ambush just as many bourgeois interests.

All the preceding classes that got the upper hand sought to fortify their already acquired status by subjecting society at large to their conditions of appropriation. The proletarians cannot become masters of the productive forces of society, except by abolishing their own previous mode of appropriation, and thereby also every other previous mode of appropriation. They have nothing of their own to secure and to fortify; their mission is to destroy all previous securities for, and insurances of, individual property.

All previous historical movements were movements of minorities, or in the interest of minorities.

Bourgeois and Proletarians

The proletarian movement is the self-conscious, independent movement of the immense majority, in the interest of the immense majority. The proletariat, the lowest stratum of our present society, cannot stir, cannot raise itself up, without the whole superincumbent strata of official society being sprung into the air.

Though not in substance, yet in form, the struggle of the proletariat with the bourgeoisie is at first a national struggle. The proletariat of each country must, of course, first of all settle matters with its own bourgeoisie.

In depicting the most general phases of the development of the proletariat, we traced the more or less veiled civil war, raging within existing society, up to the point where that war breaks out into open revolution, and where the violent overthrow of the bourgeoisie lays the foundation for the sway of the proletariat.

Hitherto, every form of society has been based, as we have already seen, on the antagonism of oppressing and oppressed classes. But in order to oppress a class, certain conditions must be assured to it under which it can, at least, continue its slavish existence. The serf, in the period of serfdom, raised himself to membership in the commune, just as the petty bourgeois, under the yoke of feudal absolutism, managed to develop into a bourgeois. The modern laborer, on the contrary, instead of rising with the progress of industry, sinks deeper and deeper below the conditions of existence of his own class. He becomes a pauper, and pauperism develops more rapidly than population and wealth. And here it becomes evident that the bourgeoisie is unfit any longer to be the ruling class in society, and to impose its conditions of existence upon society as an overriding law. It is unfit to rule because it is incompetent to assure an existence to its slave within his slavery, because it cannot help letting him sink into such a state, that it has to feed him, instead of being fed by him. Society can no longer live under this bourgeoisie, in other words, its existence is no longer compatible with society.

The essential condition for the existence, and for the sway of the bourgeois class, is the formation and augmentation of capital; the condition for capital is wage labor. Wage labor rests exclusively on competition between the laborers. The advance of industry, whose involuntary promoter is the bourgeoisie, replaces the isolation of the laborers, due to competition, by their revolutionary combination, due to association. The development of modern industry, therefore, cuts from under its feet the very foundation on which the bourgeoisie produces and appropriates products. What the bourgeoisie, therefore, produces, above all, is its own grave-diggers. Its fall and the victory of the proletariat are equally inevitable.

II

Proletarians
and Communists

In what relation do the Communists stand to the proletarians as a whole?

The Communists do not form a separate party opposed to other working-class parties.

They have no interests separate and apart from those of the proletariat as a whole.

They do not set up any sectarian principles of their own, by which to shape and mold the proletarian movement.

The Communists are distinguished from the other working-class parties by this only: 1. In the national struggles of the proletarians of the different countries, they point out and bring to the front the common interests of the entire proletariat, independently of all nationality. 2. In the various stages of development that the struggle of the working class against the bourgeoisie has to pass through, they always and everywhere represent the interests of the movement as a whole.

The Communists, therefore, are on the one hand,

practically, the most advanced and resolute section of the working-class parties of every country, that section which pushes forward all others; on the other hand, theoretically, they have over the great mass of the proletariat the advantage of clearly understanding the line of march, the conditions, and the ultimate general results of the proletarian movement.

The immediate aim of the Communists is the same as that of all the other proletarian parties: formation of the proletariat into a class, overthrow of the bourgeois supremacy, conquest of political power by the proletariat.

The theoretical conclusions of the Communists are in no way based on ideas or principles that have been invented, or discovered, by this or that would-be universal reformer.

They merely express, in general terms, actual relations springing from an existing class struggle, from a historical movement going on under our very eyes. The abolition of existing property relations is not at all a distinctive feature of communism.

All property relations in the past have continually been subject to historical change consequent upon the change in historical conditions.

The French Revolution, for example, abolished feudal property in favor of bourgeois property.

The distinguishing feature of communism is not

the abolition of property generally, but the abolition of bourgeois property. But modern bourgeois private property is the final and most complete expression of the system of producing and appropriating products that is based on class antagonisms, on the exploitation of the many by the few.

In this sense, the theory of the Communists may be summed up in the single phrase: Abolition of private property.

We Communists have been reproached with the desire of abolishing the right of personally acquiring property as the fruit of a man's own labor, which property is alleged to be the groundwork of all personal freedom, activity, and independence.

Hard-won, self-acquired, self-earned property! Do you mean the property of the petty artisan and of the small peasant, a form of property that preceded the bourgeois form? There is no need to abolish that; the development of industry has to a great extent already destroyed it, and is still destroying it daily.

Or do you mean modern bourgeois private property?

But does wage labor create any property for the laborer? Not a bit. It creates capital, *i.e.,* that kind of property that exploits wage labor, and that cannot increase except upon condition of begetting a new supply of wage labor for fresh exploitation.

Property, in its present form, is based on the antagonism of capital and wage labor. Let us examine both sides of this antagonism.

To be a capitalist, is to have not only a purely personal, but a social *status* in production. Capital is a collective product, and only by the united action of many members, nay, in the last resort, only by the united action of all members of society, can it be set in motion.

Capital is, therefore, not a personal, it is a social power.

When, therefore, capital is converted into common property, into the property of all members of society, personal property is not thereby transformed into social property. It is only the social character of the property that is changed. It loses its class character.

Let us now take wage labor.

The average price of wage labor is the minimum wage, *i.e.,* that quantum of the means of subsistence, which is absolutely requisite to keep the laborer in bare existence as a laborer. What, therefore, the wage laborer appropriates by means of his labor, merely suffices to prolong and reproduce a bare existence. We by no means intend to abolish this personal appropriation of the products of labor, an appropriation that is made for the maintenance and reproduction of human life, and that leaves no surplus wherewith to command the labor of others. All that we want to do away with is the miserable character of this appropriation, under which the laborer lives merely to increase capital, and is allowed to live only in so far as the interest of the ruling class requires it.

In bourgeois society, living labor is but a means to increase accumulated labor. In communist society, accumulated labor is but a means to widen, to enrich, to promote the existence of the laborer.

In bourgeois society, therefore, the past dominates the present; in communist society, the present dominates the past. In bourgeois society capital is independent and has individuality, while the living person is dependent and has no individuality.

And the abolition of this state of things is called by the bourgeoisie, abolition of individuality and freedom! And rightly so. The abolition of bourgeois individuality, bourgeois independence, and bourgeois freedom is undoubtedly aimed at.

By freedom is meant, under the present bourgeois conditions of production, free trade, free selling and buying.

But if selling and buying disappears, free selling and buying disappears also. This talk about free selling and buying, and all the other "brave words" of our bourgeoisie about freedom in general, have a meaning, if any, only in contrast with restricted selling and buying, with the fettered traders of the Middle Ages, but have no meaning when opposed to the communistic abolition of buying and selling, of the bourgeois conditions of production, and of the bourgeoisie itself.

You are horrified at our intending to do away with private property. But in your existing society, private property is already done away with for nine-tenths of the population; its existence for the few is solely due to its non-existence in the hands of those nine-tenths. You reproach us, therefore, with intending to do away with a form of property, the necessary condition for whose existence is the non-existence of any property for the immense majority of society.

In one word, you reproach us with intending to do away with your property. Precisely so; that is just what we intend.

From the moment when labor can no longer be converted into capital, money, or rent, into a social power capable of being monopolized, *i.e.*, from the moment when individual property can no longer be transformed into bourgeois property, into capital, from that moment, you say, individuality vanishes.

You must, therefore, confess that by "individual" you mean no other person than the bourgeois, than the middle-class owner of property. This person must, indeed, be swept out of the way, and made impossible.

Communism deprives no man of the power to appropriate the products of society; all that it does is to deprive him of the power to subjugate the labor of others by means of such appropriation.

It has been objected that upon the abolition of private property all work will cease, and universal laziness will overtake us.

According to this, bourgeois society ought long ago to have gone to the dogs through sheer idleness; for those of its members who work, acquire nothing, and those who acquire anything, do not work. The whole of this objection is but another expression of the tautology: that there can no longer be any wage labor when there is no longer any capital.

All objections urged against the communistic mode of producing and appropriating material products, have, in the same way, been urged against the communistic modes of producing and appropriating intellectual products. Just as, to the bourgeois, the disappearance of class property is the disappearance of production itself, so the disappearance of class culture is to him identical with the disappearance of all culture.

That culture, the loss of which he laments, is, for the enormous majority, a mere training to act as a machine.

But don't wrangle with us so long as you apply, to our intended abolition of bourgeois property, the standard of your bourgeois notions of freedom, culture, law, etc. Your very ideas are but the outgrowth of the conditions of your bourgeois production and bourgeois property, just as your jurisprudence is but the will of your class made into a law for all, a will whose essential character and direction are determined by the economical conditions of existence of your class.

The selfish misconception that induces you to transform into eternal laws of nature and of reason the social forms springing from your present mode of production and form of property—historical relations that rise and disappear in the progress of production—this misconception you share with every ruling class that has preceded you. What you see clearly in the case of ancient property, what you admit in the case of feudal property, you are of course forbidden to admit in the case of your own bourgeois form of property.

Abolition of the family! Even the most radical flare up at this infamous proposal of the Communists.

On what foundation is the present family, the bourgeois family, based? On capital, on private gain. In its completely developed form this family exists only among the bourgeoisie. But this state of things finds its complement in the practical absence of the family among the proletarians, and in public prostitution.

The bourgeois family will vanish as a matter of course when its complement vanishes, and both will vanish with the vanishing of capital.

Do you charge us with wanting to stop the exploitation of children by their parents? To this crime we plead guilty.

But, you will say, we destroy the most hallowed of relations, when we replace home education by social.

And your education! Is not that also social, and determined by the social conditions under which you educate, by the intervention, direct or indirect, of society, by means of schools, etc.? The Communists have not invented the intervention of society in education; they merely seek to alter the character of that intervention, and to rescue education from the influence of the ruling class.

The bourgeois clap-trap about the family and education, about the hallowed co-relation of parent and child, becomes all the more disgusting; the more, by the action of modern industry, all family ties among the proletarians are torn asunder, and their children transformed into simple articles of commerce and instruments of labor.

Proletarians and Communists

But you Communists would introduce free love,[1] screams the whole bourgeoisie in chorus.

The bourgeois sees in his wife a mere instrument of production. He hears that the instruments of production are to be exploited in common, and, naturally, can come to no other conclusion than that the lot of being common to all will likewise fall to the women.

He has not even a suspicion that the real point aimed at is to do away with the status of women as mere instruments of production.

For the rest, nothing is more ridiculous than the virtuous indignation of our bourgeois at free love which, they pretend, is to be openly and officially established by the Communists. The Communists have no need to introduce free love; it has existed almost from time immemorial.

Our bourgeoisie, not content with having the wives and daughters of their proletarians at their disposal, not to speak of common prostitutes, take supreme delight in seducing each other's wives.

Bourgeois marriage is in reality a system of wives in common and thus, at the most, what the Communists might possibly be reproached with, is that they desire to introduce, in substitution for a hypocritically concealed, an openly legalized system of free love.

---

[1] *Weibergemeinschaft*, literally communal wives, in German.—*Ed.*

Moreover, it is self-evident that the abolition of the present system of production must bring with it the abolition of free love springing from that system, *i.e.,* of prostitution both public and private.

The Communists are further reproached with desiring to abolish countries and nationality.

The workingmen have no country. We cannot take from them what they have not got. Since the proletariat must first of all acquire political supremacy, must rise to be the leading class of the nation, must constitute itself *the* nation, it is, so far, itself national, though not in the bourgeois sense of the word.

National differences and antagonisms between peoples are daily vanishing, owing to the development of the bourgeoisie, to freedom of commerce, to the world market, to uniformity in the mode of production and in the conditions of life corresponding thereto.

The supremacy of the proletariat will cause them to vanish still faster. United action, of the leading civilized countries at least, is one of the first conditions for the emancipation of the proletariat.

In proportion as the exploitation of one individual by another is put to an end, the exploitation of one nation by another will also be put to an end. In proportion as the antagonism between classes within the nation vanishes, the hostility of one nation to another will come to an end.

The charges against communism made from a religious, a philosophical, and, generally, from an ideological standpoint are not deserving of serious examination.

Does it require deep intuition to comprehend that man's ideas, views and conceptions, in one word, man's consciousness, changes with every change in the conditions of his material existence, in his social relations and in his social life?

What else does the history of ideas prove, than that intellectual production changes its character in proportion as material production is changed? The ruling ideas of each age have ever been the ideas of its ruling class.

When people speak of ideas that revolutionize society, they do but express the fact that within the old society the elements of a new one have been created, and that the dissolution of the old ideas keeps even pace with the dissolution of the old conditions of existence.

When the ancient world was in its last throes, the ancient religions were overcome by Christianity. When Christian ideas succumbed in the eighteenth century to rationalist ideas, feudal society fought its death battle with the then revolutionary bourgeoisie. The ideas of religious liberty and freedom of conscience merely gave expression to the sway of free competition within the domain of knowledge.

Undoubtedly, it will be said, religious, moral, philosophical, and juridical ideas have been modified in the course of historical development. But religion, morality, philosophy, political science, and law constantly survived this change.

There are, besides, eternal truths, such as Freedom, Justice, etc., that are common to all states of society. But communism abolishes eternal truths, it abolishes all religion, and all morality, instead of constituting them on a new basis; it therefore acts in contradiction to all past historical experience.

What does this accusation reduce itself to? The history of all past society has consisted in the development of class antagonisms, antagonisms that assumed different forms at different epochs.

But whatever form they may have taken, one fact is common to all past ages, *viz.,* the exploitation of one part of society by the other. No wonder, then, that the social consciousness of past ages, despite all the multiplicity and variety it displays, moves within certain common forms, or general ideas, which cannot completely vanish except with the total disappearance of class antagonisms.

The communist revolution is the most radical rupture with traditional property relations; no wonder that its development involves the most radical rupture with traditional ideas.

But let us have done with the bourgeois objections to communism.

We have seen above that the first step in the revolution by the working class is to raise the proletariat to the position of ruling class to win the battle of democracy.

The proletariat will use its political supremacy to wrest, by degrees, all capital from the bourgeoisie, to centralize all instruments of production in the hands of the state, *i.e.,* of the proletariat organized as the ruling class; and to increase the total of productive forces as rapidly as possible.

Of course, in the beginning, this cannot be effected except by means of despotic inroads on the rights of property, and on the conditions of bourgeois production; by means of measures, therefore, which appear economically insufficient and untenable, but which, in the course of the movement, outstrip themselves, necessitate further inroads upon the old social order, and are unavoidable as a means of entirely revolutionizing the mode of production.

These measures will of course be different in different countries.

Nevertheless in the most advanced countries, the following will be pretty generally applicable.

1. Abolition of property in land and application of all rents of land to public purposes.

2. A heavy progressive or graduated income tax.

3. Abolition of all right of inheritance.

4. Confiscation of the property of all emigrants and rebels.

5. Centralization of credit in the hands of the state, by means of a national bank with state capital and an exclusive monopoly.

6. Centralization of the means of communication and transport in the hands of the state.

7. Extension of factories and instruments of production owned by the state; the bringing into cultivation of wastelands, and the improvement of the soil generally in accordance with a common plan.

8. Equal liability of all to labor. Establishment of industrial armies, especially for agriculture.

9. Combination of agriculture with manufacturing industries; gradual abolition of the distinction between town and country, by a more equable distribution of the population over the country.

10. Free education for all children in public schools. Abolition of children's factory labor in its present form. Combination of education with industrial production, etc., etc.

When, in the course of development, class distinctions have disappeared, and all production has been concentrated in the hands of a vast association of the whole nation, the public power will lose its political character. Political power, properly so called, is merely the organized power of one class for oppressing another. If the proletariat during its contest with the bourgeoisie is compelled, by the force of circumstances, to organize itself as a class, if, by means of a revolution, it makes itself the ruling class, and, as such, sweeps away by force the old conditions of production, then it will, along with these conditions, have swept away the conditions for the existence of class antagonisms and of classes generally, and will thereby have abolished its own supremacy as a class.

In place of the old bourgeois society, with its classes and class antagonisms, we shall have an association in which the free development of each is the condition for the free development of all.

III

Socialist and Communist Literature

1. Reactionary Socialism

A. FEUDAL SOCIALISM

OWING to their historical position, it became the vocation of the aristocracies of France and England to write pamphlets against modern bourgeois society. In the French revolution of July 1830 and in the English reform agitation these aristocracies again succumbed to the hateful upstart. Thenceforth, a serious political contest was altogether out of the question. A literary battle alone remained possible. But even in the domain of literature the old cries of the restoration period[1] had become impossible.

In order to arouse sympathy the aristocracy were obliged to lose sight, apparently, of their own in-

---

[1] Not the English Restoration 1660 to 1689, but the French Restoration 1814 to 1830. [*Note by Engels in the edition of 1888.*]

terests, and to formulate their indictment against the bourgeoisie in the interest of the exploited working class alone. Thus the aristocracy took their revenge by singing lampoons on their new master, and whispering in his ears sinister prophecies of coming catastrophe.

In this way feudal socialism arose: half lamentation, half lampoon; half echo of the past, half menace of the future; at times, by its bitter, witty and incisive criticism, striking the bourgeoisie to the very quick; but always ludicrous in its effect, through total incapacity to comprehend the march of modern history.

The aristocracy, in order to rally the people to them, waved the proletarian alms-bag in front for a banner. But the people, so often as it joined them, saw on their hindquarters the old feudal coats of arms, and deserted with loud and irreverent laughter.

One section of the French Legitimists[2] and "Young England"[3] exhibited this spectacle.

In pointing out that their mode of exploitation

---

[2] The Legitimists: The party of the noble landowners, who advocated the restoration of the Bourbon dynasty.—*Ed.*

[3] Young England: A group of British Conservatives—aristocrats and men of politics and literature—formed about 1842. Prominent among them were Disraeli, Thomas Carlyle, and others.—*Ed.*

was different from that of the bourgeoisie, the feudalists forget that they exploited under circumstances and conditions that were quite different, and that are now antiquated. In showing that, under their rule, the modern proletariat never existed, they forget that the modern bourgeoisie is the necessary offspring of their own form of society.

For the rest, so little do they conceal the reactionary character of their criticism that their chief accusation against the bourgeoisie amounts to this, that under the bourgeois regime a class is being developed, which is destined to cut up root and branch the old order of society.

What they upbraid the bourgeoisie with is not so much that it creates a proletariat, as that it creates a *revolutionary* proletariat.

In political practice, therefore, they join in all coercive measures against the working class; and in ordinary life, despite their highfalutin phrases, they stoop to pick up the golden apples dropped from the tree of industry, and to barter truth, love, and honor for traffic in wool, beetroot-sugar, and potato spirits.[4]

---

[4] This applies chiefly to Germany where the landed aristocracy and squirearchy have large portions of their estates cultivated for their own account by stewards, and are, moreover, extensive beetroot-sugar manufacturers and distillers of potato spirits. The wealthier British aristocracy are, as yet, rather above that; but they, too, know how to

As the parson has ever gone hand in hand with the landlord, so has clerical socialism with feudal socialism.

Nothing is easier than to give Christian asceticism a socialist tinge. Has not Christianity declaimed against private property, against marriage, against the state? Has it not preached in the place of these, charity and poverty, celibacy and mortification of the flesh, monastic life and Mother Church? Christian socialism is but the holy water with which the priest consecrates the vexation of the aristocrat.

B. PETTY-BOURGEOIS SOCIALISM

The feudal aristocracy was not the only class that was ruined by the bourgeoisie, not the only class whose conditions of existence pined and perished in the atmosphere of modern bourgeois society. The medieval burghers and the small farmer proprietors were the precursors of the modern bourgeoisie. In those countries that are but little developed, industrially and commercially, these two classes still vegetate side by side with the rising bourgeoisie.

In countries where modern civilization has become fully developed, a new class of petty bourgeois

---

make up for declining rents by lending their names to floaters of more or less shady joint-stock companies. [*Note by Engels in the edition of 1888.*]

has been formed, fluctuating between proletariat and bourgeoisie and ever renewing itself as a supplementary part of bourgeois society. The individual members of this class, however, are being constantly hurled down into the proletariat by the action of competition, and, as modern industry develops, they even see the moment approaching when they will completely disappear as an independent section of modern society, to be replaced in manufactures, agriculture, and commerce by overlookers, bailiffs, and shopmen.

In countries like France, where the farmers constitute far more than half of the population, it was natural that writers who sided with the proletariat against the bourgeoisie, should use, in their criticism of the bourgeois regime, the standard of the farmer and petty bourgeois, and from the standpoint of these intermediate classes should take up the cudgels for the working class. Thus arose petty-bourgeois socialism. Sismondi was the head of this school, not only in France but also in England.

This school of socialism dissected with great acuteness the contradictions in the conditions of modern production. It laid bare the hypocritical apologies of economists. It proved, incontrovertibly, the disastrous effects of machinery and division of labor, the concentration of capital and land in a few hands, over-production and crises; it pointed out the inevitable ruin of the petty bourgeois and farmer, the misery of the proletariat, the anarchy in production, the crying inequalities in the distribution of wealth, the industrial war of extermination between nations, the dissolution of old moral bonds, of the old family relations, of the old nationalities.

In its positive aims, however, this form of socialism aspires either to restoring the old means of production and of exchange, and with them the old property relations and the old society, or to cramping the modern means of production and of exchange within the framework of the old property relations that have been, and were bound to be, exploded by those means. In either case, it is both reactionary and Utopian.

Its last words are: corporate guilds for manufacture; patriarchal relations in agriculture.

Ultimately, when stubborn historical facts had dispersed all intoxicating effects of self-deception, this form of socialism ended in a miserable hangover.

C. GERMAN OR "TRUE" SOCIALISM

The socialist and communist literature of France, a literature that originated under the pressure of a bourgeoisie in power, and that was the expression of the struggle against this power, was introduced into Germany at a time when the bourgeoisie in that country had just begun its contest with feudal absolutism.

German philosophers, would-be philosophers, *beaux esprits* eagerly seized on this literature, only forgetting that when these writings immigrated from France into Germany, French social conditions had not immigrated along with them. In contact with German social conditions this French literature lost all its immediate practical significance and assumed a purely literary aspect. Thus, to the German philosophers of the eighteenth century, the demands of the first French revolution were nothing more than the demands of "Practical Reason" in general, and the utterance of the will of the revolutionary French bourgeoisie signified in their eyes the laws of pure Will, of Will as it was bound to be, of true human Will generally.

The work of the German *literati* consisted solely in bringing the new French ideas into harmony with their ancient philosophical conscience, or rather, in annexing the French ideas without deserting their own philosophic point of view.

This annexation took place in the same way in which a foreign language is appropriated, namely, by translation.

It is well known how the monks wrote silly lives

of Catholic Saints *over* the manuscripts on which
the classical works of ancient pagan civilization had
been written. The German *literati* reversed this process with the profane French literature. They wrote
their philosophical nonsense beneath the French
original. For instance, beneath the French criticism
of the economic functions of money, they wrote
"Alienation of Humanity," and beneath the French
criticism of the bourgeois state they wrote, "De-
thronement of the Category of the General," and so
forth.

The introduction of these philosophical phrases
at the back of the French historical criticisms they
dubbed "Philosophy of Action," "True Socialism,"
"German Science of Socialism," "Philosophical
Foundation of Socialism," and so on.

The French socialist and communist literature
was thus completely emasculated. And, since it
ceased in the hands of a German to express the
struggle of one class with the other, he felt conscious
of having overcome "French one-sidedness" and of
representing not true requirements, but the requirements of Truth; not the interests of the proletariat,
but the interests of Human Nature, of Man in general, who belongs to no class, has no reality, who
exists only in the misty realm of philosophical fan-
tasy.

This German socialism, which took its schoolboy

task so seriously and solemnly and extolled its poor stock-in-trade in such mountebank fashion, meanwhile gradually lost its pedantic innocence.

The fight of the German, and, especially, of the Prussian bourgeoisie, against feudal aristocracy and absolute monarchy, in other words, the liberal movement, became more earnest.

Thus, the long wished-for opportunity was offered to "True" socialism of confronting the political movement with the socialist demands, of hurling the traditional anathemas against liberalism, against representative government, against bourgeois competition, bourgeois freedom of the press, bourgeois legislation, bourgeois liberty and equality, and of preaching to the masses that they had nothing to gain and everything to lose by this bourgeois movement. German socialism forgot, in the nick of time, that the French criticism, whose silly echo it was, presupposed the existence of modern bourgeois society, with its corresponding economic conditions of existence and the political constitution adapted thereto, the very things whose attainment was the object of the pending struggle in Germany.

To the absolute governments, with their following of parsons, professors, country squires and officials, it served as a welcome scarecrow against the threatening bourgeoisie.

It was a sweet finish after the bitter pills of floggings and bullets with which these same governments, just at that time, dosed the German working-class risings.

While this "True" socialism thus served the governments as a weapon for fighting the German bourgeoisie, it, at the same time, directly represented a reactionary interest, the interest of the German petty-bourgeoisie. In Germany the petty-bourgeois class, a relic of the sixteenth century, and since then constantly cropping up again under various forms, is the real social basis of the existing state of things.

To preserve this class is to preserve the existing state of things in Germany. The industrial and political supremacy of the bourgeoisie threatens it with certain destruction, on the one hand from the concentration of capital, on the other from the rise of a revolutionary proletariat. "True" socialism appeared to kill these two birds with one stone. It spread like an epidemic.

The robe of speculative cobwebs, embroidered with flowers of rhetoric, steeped in the dew of sickly sentiment, this transcendental robe in which the German socialists wrapped their sorry "eternal truths," all skin and bone, served to wonderfully increase the sale of their goods amongst such a public.

And on its part, German socialism recognized, more and more, its own calling as the bombastic representative of the petty-bourgeois Philistine.

It proclaimed the German nation to be the model nation, and the German petty Philistine to be the typical man. To every villainous meanness of this model man it gave a hidden, higher, socialistic interpretation, the exact contrary of its real character. It went to the extreme length of directly opposing the "brutally destructive" tendency of communism, and of proclaiming its supreme and impartial contempt of all class struggles. With very few exceptions, all the so-called socialist and communist publications that now (1847) circulate in Germany belong to the domain of this foul and enervating literature.[5]

2. Conservative or Bourgeois Socialism

A part of the bourgeoisie is desirous of redressing social grievances, in order to secure the continued existence of bourgeois society.

To this section belong economists, philanthropists, humanitarians, improvers of the condition of the working class, organizers of charity, members of

---

[5] The revolutionary storm of 1848 swept away this whole shabby tendency and cured its protagonists of the desire to dabble further in socialism. The chief representative and classical type of this tendency is Herr Karl Grün. [*Note by Engels in the edition of 1890.*]

societies for the prevention of cruelty to animals, temperance fanatics, hole-and-corner reformers of every imaginable kind. This form of socialism has, moreover, been worked out into complete systems.

We may cite Proudhon's *Philosophie de la Misère* as an example of this form.

The socialistic bourgeois want all the advantages of modern social conditions without the struggles and dangers necessarily resulting therefrom. They desire the existing state of society minus its revolutionary and disintegrating elements. They wish for a bourgeoisie without a proletariat. The bourgeoisie naturally conceives the world in which it is supreme to be the best; and bourgeois socialism develops this comfortable conception into various more or less complete systems. In requiring the proletariat to carry out such a system, and thereby to march straightway into the social New Jerusalem, it but requires in reality that the proletariat should remain within the bounds of existing society, but should cast away all its hateful ideas concerning the bourgeoisie.

A second and more practical, but less systematic, form of this socialism sought to depreciate every revolutionary movement in the eyes of the working class by showing that no mere political reform, but only a change in the material conditions of existence, in economical relations, could be of any advantage to them. By changes in the material conditions of existence, this form of socialism, however, by no means understands abolition of the bourgeois relations of production, an abolition that can be effected only by a revolution, but administrative reforms based on the continued existence of these relations; reforms, therefore, that in no respect affect the relations between capital and labor, but, at the best, lessen the cost and simplify the administrative work of bourgeois government.

Bourgeois socialism attains adequate expression, when, and only when, it becomes a mere figure of speech.

Free trade: for the benefit of the working class. Protective duties: for the benefit of the working class. Prison Reform: for the benefit of the working class. This is the last word and the only seriously meant word of bourgeois socialism.

It is summed up in the phrase: the bourgeois is a bourgeois—for the benefit of the working class.

3. Critical-Utopian Socialism and Communism

We do not here refer to that literature which, in every great modern revolution, has always given voice to the demands of the proletariat, such as the writings of Babeuf and others.

The first direct attempts of the proletariat to attain its own ends, made in times of universal excitement when feudal society was being overthrown, necessarily failed, owing to the then undeveloped state of the proletariat, as well as to the absence of the economic conditions for its emancipation, conditions that had yet to be produced, and could be produced by the impending bourgeois epoch alone. The revolutionary literature that accompanied these first movements of the proletariat had necessarily a reactionary character. It inculcated universal asceticism and social leveling in its crudest form.

The socialist and communist systems properly so called, those of St. Simon, Fourier, Owen, and others spring into existence in the early undeveloped period, described above, of the struggle between proletariat and bourgeoisie (see Section I. "Bourgeois and Proletarians").

The founders of these systems see, indeed, the class antagonisms, as well as the action of the decomposing elements in the prevailing form of society. But the proletariat, as yet in its infancy, offers to them the spectacle of a class without any historical initiative or any independent political movement.

Since the development of class antagonism keeps even pace with the development of industry, the economic situation, as they find it, does not as yet offer to them the material conditions for the emancipation of the proletariat. They therefore search after a new social science, after new social laws that are to create these conditions.

Historical action is to yield to their personal inventive action, historically created conditions of emancipation to fantastic ones; and the gradual, spontaneous class organization of the proletariat to an organization of society specially contrived by these inventors. Future history resolves itself, in their eyes, into the propaganda and the practical carrying out of their social plans.

In the formation of their plans they are conscious of caring chiefly for the interests of the working class as being the most suffering class. Only from the point of view of being the most suffering class does the proletariat exist for them.

The undeveloped state of the class struggle, as well as their own surroundings, causes socialists of this kind to consider themselves far superior to all class antagonisms. They want to improve the condition of every member of society, even that of the most favored. Hence, they habitually appeal to society at large, without distinction of class; nay, by preference, to the ruling class. For how can people, when once they understand their system, fail to see in it the best possible plan of the best possible state of society?

Hence, they reject all political, and especially all revolutionary, action; they wish to attain their ends by peaceful means, and endeavor, by small experiments necessarily doomed to failure, and by the force of example, to pave the way for the new social gospel.

Such fantastic pictures of future society, painted at a time when the proletariat is still in a very undeveloped state and has but a fantastic conception of its own position, correspond with the first instinctive yearnings of that class for a general reconstruction of society.

But these socialist and communist publications contain also a critical element. They attack every principle of existing society. Hence they are full of the most valuable materials for the enlightenment of the working class. The practical measures proposed in them—such as the abolition of the distinction between town and country, of the family, of the carrying on of industries for the account of private individuals, and of the wage system, the proclamation of social harmony, the conversion of the functions of the state into a mere superintendence of production—all these proposals point solely to the disappearance of class antagonisms which were, at that time, only just cropping up, and which, in these publications, are recognized in their earliest indistinct and undefined forms only. These proposals, therefore, are of a purely Utopian character.

The significance of Critical-Utopian socialism and communism bears an inverse relation to historical development. In proportion as the modern class struggle develops and takes definite shape, this fantastic standing apart from the contest, these fantastic attacks on it, lose all practical value and all theoretical justification. Therefore, although the originators of these systems were, in many respects, revolutionary, their disciples have, in every case, formed mere reactionary sects. They hold fast by the original views of their masters, in opposition to the progressive historical development of the proletariat. They, therefore, endeavor, and that consistently, to deaden the class struggle and to reconcile the class antagonisms. They still dream of experimental realization of their social Utopias, of founding isolated *"phalanstères,"* of establishing "Home Colonies," of setting up a "Little Icaria"[6]—duodecimo editions of the New Jerusalem—and to real-

---

[6] *Phalanstères* were socialist colonies on the plan of Charles Fourier; *Icaria* was the name given by Cabet to his Utopia and, later on, to his American communist colony. [*Note by Engels in the edition of 1888.*]

Home colonies were what Owen called his communist model societies. [*Note by Engels in the edition of 1890.*]

ize all these castles in the air, they are compelled to appeal to the feelings and purses of the bourgeois. By degrees they sink into the category of the reactionary conservative socialists depicted above, differing from these only by more systematic pedantry, and by their fanatical and superstitious belief in the miraculous effects of their social science.

They, therefore, violently oppose all political action on the part of the working class; such action, according to them, can only result from blind unbelief in the new gospel.

The Owenites in England, and the Fourierists in France, respectively oppose the Chartists and the *Réformistes.*[7]

---

[7] This refers to the adherents of the newspaper *La Réforme*, which was published in Paris from 1843 to 1850. —*Ed.*

IV

Position of the Communists in Relation to the Various Existing Opposition Parties

SECTION II has made clear the relations of the Communists to the existing working-class parties, such as the Chartists in England and the Agrarian Reformers in America.

The Communists fight for the attainment of the immediate aims, for the enforcement of the momentary interests of the working class; but in the movement of the present, they also represent and take care of the future of that movement. In France the Communists ally themselves with the Social-Democrats,[1] against the conservative and radical bourgeoisie, reserving, however, the right to take up a critical position in regard to phrases and il-

---

[1] The party then represented in Parliament by Ledru-Rollin, in literature by Louis Blanc, in the daily press by the *Réforme*. The name of Social-Democracy signified, with these its inventors, a section of the Democratic or Republican party more or less tinged with socialism. [*Note by Engels in the edition of 1888.*]

lusions traditionally handed down from the great revolution.

In Switzerland they support the radicals, without losing sight of the fact that this party consists of antagonistic elements, partly of Democratic Socialists, in the French sense, partly of radical bourgeois.

In Poland they support the party that insists on an agrarian revolution as the prime condition for national emancipation, that party which fomented the insurrection of Cracow in 1846.

In Germany they fight with the bourgeoisie whenever it acts in a revolutionary way, against the absolute monarchy, the feudal squirearchy, and the petty bourgeoisie.[2]

But they never cease, for a single instant, to instill into the working class the clearest possible recognition of the hostile antagonism between bourgeoisie and proletariat, in order that the German workers may straightway use, as so many weapons against the bourgeoisie, the social and political conditions that the bourgeoisie must necessarily introduce along with its supremacy, and in order that, after the fall of the reactionary classes in Germany, the fight against the bourgeoisie itself may immediately begin.

---

[2] *Kleinbürgerei* in the German original. Marx and Engels used this term to describe the reactionary elements of the urban petty bourgeoisie.—*Ed.*

115

The Communists turn their attention chiefly to Germany, because that country is on the eve of a bourgeois revolution that is bound to be carried out under more advanced conditions of European civilization, and with a much more developed proletariat, than that of England was in the seventeenth, and of France in the eighteenth century, and because the bourgeois revolution in Germany will be but the prelude to an immediately following proletarian revolution.

In short, the Communists everywhere support every revolutionary movement against the existing social and political order of things.

In all these movements they bring to the front, as the leading question in each, the property question, no matter what its degree of development at the time.

Finally, they labor everywhere for the union and agreement of the democratic parties of all countries.

The Communists disdain to conceal their views and aims. They openly declare that their ends can be attained only by the forcible overthrow of all existing social conditions. Let the ruling classes tremble at a Communistic revolution. The proletarians have nothing to lose but their chains. They have a world to win.

WORKINGMEN OF ALL COUNTRIES, UNITE!

ADDENDA

Preface to the
German Edition of 1872

THE Communist League, an international association of workers, which could of course be only a secret one under the conditions obtaining at the time, commissioned the undersigned, at the Congress held in London in November 1847, to draw up for publication a detailed theoretical and practical program of the party. Such was the origin of the following *Manifesto,* the manuscript of which traveled to London, to be printed, a few weeks before the February revolution.[1] First published in German, it has been republished in that language in at least twelve different editions in Germany, England, and America. It was published in English for the first time in 1850 in the *Red Republican,* London, translated by Miss Helen Macfarlane, and in 1871 in at least three different translations in America. A French version first appeared in Paris shortly before the June insurrection of 1848 and

---

[1] The February revolution in France, 1848.—*Ed.*

recently in *Le Socialiste* of New York. A new translation is in the course of preparation. A Polish version appeared in London shortly after it was first published in German. A Russian translation was published in Geneva in the sixties. Into Danish, too, it was translated shortly after its first appearance.

However much the state of things may have altered during the last twenty-five years, the general principles laid down in this *Manifesto* are, on the whole, as correct today as ever. Here and there some detail might be improved. The practical application of the principles will depend, as the *Manifesto* itself states, everywhere and at all times, on the historical conditions existing at the time, and, for that reason, no special stress is laid on the revolutionary measures proposed at the end of Section II. That passage would, in many respects, be very differently worded today. In view of the gigantic strides of modern industry in the last twenty-five years, and of the accompanying improved and extended party organization of the working class, in view of the practical experience gained, first in the February revolution, and then, still more, in the Paris Commune, where the proletariat for the first time held political power for two whole months, this program has in some details become antiquated. One thing especially was proved by the Commune, *viz.*, that "the working class cannot simply lay hold of the ready-made state machinery and wield it for its own purposes." (See *The Civil War in France; Address of the General Council of the International Working Men's Association*, London, Truelove, 1871, p. 15, where this point is further developed.[2]) Further, it is self-evident that the criticism of socialist literature is deficient in relation to the present time, because it comes down only to 1847; also, that the remarks on the relation of the Communists to the various opposition parties (Section IV), although in principle still correct, yet in practice are antiquated, because the political situation has been entirely changed, and the progress of history has swept from off the earth the greater portion of the political parties there enumerated.

But, then, the *Manifesto* has become a historical document which we have no longer any right to alter. A subsequent edition may perhaps appear with an introduction bridging the gap from 1847 to the present day; this reprint was too unexpected to leave us time for that.

Karl Marx   Friedrich Engels

London, June 24, 1872

---

[2] K. Marx and F. Engels, *Selected Works*, 2 vols., Vol. I, Moscow, 1951, p. 468 ff.—*Ed.*

Preface to the
Russian Edition of 1882

THE first Russian edition of the *Manifesto of the Communist Party,* translated by Bakunin, was published early in the sixties[1] by the printing office of the *Kolokol.* Then the West could see in it (the Russian edition of the *Manifesto*) only a literary curiosity. Such a view would be impossible today.

What a limited field the proletarian movement still occupied at that time (December, 1847) is most clearly shown by the last section of the *Manifesto:* the position of the Communists in relation to the various opposition parties in the various countries. Precisely Russia and the United States are missing here. It was the time when Russia constituted the last great reserve of all European reaction, when the United States absorbed the surplus proletarian forces of Europe through immigration.

---

[1] The edition referred to appeared in 1869. In Engels' Preface in the edition of 1888, the publication date of this Russian translation of the *Manifesto* is also incorrectly given.—*Ed.*

122

Both countries provided Europe with raw materials, and were at the same time markets for the sale of its industrial products. At that time both were, therefore, in one way or another, pillars of the existing European order.

How very different today! European immigration fitted North America for a gigantic agricultural production, whose competition is shaking the very foundations of European landed property—large and small. In addition it enabled the United States to exploit its tremendous industrial resources with an energy and on a scale that must shortly break the industrial monopoly of Western Europe, and especially of England, existing up to now. Both circumstances react in revolutionary manner upon America itself. Step by step the small and middle landownership of the farmers, the basis of the whole political constitution, is succumbing to the competition of giant farms; simultaneously, a mass proletariat and a fabulous concentration of capital are developing for the first time in the industrial regions.

And now Russia! During the Revolution of 1848-49 not only the European princes, but the European bourgeois as well, found their only salvation from the proletariat, just beginning to awaken, in Russian intervention. The tsar was proclaimed the chief of European reaction. Today he is a prisoner of war of the revolution, in Gatchina, and Russia forms the vanguard of revolutionary action in Europe.

The *Communist Manifesto* had as its object the proclamation of the inevitably impending dissolution of modern bourgeois property. But in Russia we find, face to face with the rapidly developing capitalist swindle and bourgeois landed property, just beginning to develop, more than half the land owned in common by the peasants. Now the question is: can the Russian *obshchina*,[2] though greatly undermined, yet a form of the primeval common ownership of land, pass directly to the higher form of communist common ownership? Or on the contrary, must it first pass through the same process of dissolution as constitutes the historical evolution of the West?

The only answer to that possible today is this: If the Russian revolution becomes the signal for a proletarian revolution in the West, so that both complement each other, the present Russian common ownership of land may serve as the starting point for a communist development.

Karl Marx   *Friedrich Engels*

London, January 21, 1882

---

[2] *Obshchina:* Village community.—*Ed.*

Preface to the
German Edition of 1883

THE preface to the present edition I must, alas, sign alone. Marx, the man to whom the whole working class of Europe and America owes more than to anyone else—rests at Highgate Cemetery and over his grave the first grass is already growing. Since his death, there can be even less thought of revising or supplementing the *Manifesto*. All the more do I consider it necessary again to state the following:

The basic thought running through the *Manifesto* —that economic production and the structure of society of every historical epoch necessarily arising therefrom constitute the foundation for the political and intellectual history of that epoch; that consequently (ever since the dissolution of the primeval communal ownership of land) all history has been a history of class struggles, of struggles between exploited and exploiting, between dominated and dominating classes at various stages of social development; that this struggle, however, has now reached a stage where the exploited and oppressed class (the proletariat) can no longer emancipate itself from the class which exploits and oppresses it (the bourgeoisie), without at the same time forever freeing the whole of society from exploitation, oppression, and class struggles—this basic thought belongs solely and exclusively to Marx.[1]

I have already stated this many times; but precisely now it is necessary that it also stand in front of the *Manifesto* itself.

Friedrich Engels

London, June 28, 1883

---

[1] "This proposition," I wrote in the preface to the English translation, "which, in my opinion, is destined to do for history what Darwin's theory has done for biology, we, both of us, had been gradually approaching for some years before 1845. How far I had independently progressed toward it, is best shown by my *Condition of the Working Class in England*. But when I again met Marx at Brussels, in spring, 1845, he had it ready worked out, and put it before me, in terms almost as clear as those in which I have stated it here." [*Note by Engels in the edition of 1890.*]

Preface to the
German Edition of 1890

SINCE the above was written,[1] a new German edition of the *Manifesto* has again become necessary, and much has also happened to the *Manifesto* which should be recorded here.

A second Russian translation—by Vera Zasulich —appeared at Geneva in 1882; the preface to that edition was written by Marx and myself. Unfortunately, the original German manuscript has gone astray; I must therefore retranslate from the Russian, which will in no way improve the text. It reads:

The first Russian edition of the *Manifesto of the Communist Party,* translated by Bakunin, was published early in the sixties by the printing office of the *Kolokol.* Then the West could see in it (the Russian edition of the *Manifesto*) only a literary curiosity. Such a view would be impossible today.

---

[1] Engels is referring to his preface in the edition of 1883.—*Ed.*

Addenda

What a limited field the proletarian movement still occupied at that time (December, 1847) is most clearly shown by the last section of the *Manifesto:* the position of the Communists in relation to the various opposition parties in the various countries. Precisely Russia and the United States are missing here. It was the time when Russia constituted the last great reserve of all European reaction, when the United States absorbed the surplus proletarian forces of Europe through immigration. Both countries provided Europe with raw materials, and were at the same time markets for the sale of its industrial products. At that time both were, therefore, in one way or another, pillars of the existing European order.

How very different today! European immigration fitted North America for a gigantic agricultural production, whose competition is shaking the very foundations of European landed property—large and small. In addition it enabled the United States to exploit its tremendous industrial resources with an energy and on a scale that must shortly break the industrial monopoly of Western Europe, and especially of England, existing up to now. Both circumstances react in revolutionary manner

128

upon America itself. Step by step the small and middle landownership of the farmers, the basis of the whole political constitution, is succumbing to the competition of giant farms; simultaneously, a mass proletariat and a fabulous concentration of capital are developing for the first time in the industrial regions.

And now Russia! During the revolution of 1848-49 not only the European princes, but the European bourgeois as well, found their only salvation from the proletariat, just beginning to awaken, in Russian intervention. The tsar was proclaimed the chief of European reaction. Today he is a prisoner of war of the revolution, in Gatchina, and Russia forms the vanguard of revolutionary action in Europe.

The Communist Manifesto had as its object the proclamation of the inevitably impending dissolution of modern bourgeois property. But in Russia we find, face to face with the rapidly developing capitalist swindle and bourgeois landed property, just beginning to develop, more than half the land owned in common by the peasants. Now the question is: can the Russian *obshchina,* though greatly undermined, yet a form of the primeval common ownership of land, pass directly to the higher form of communist common ownership? Or on the contrary, must it first pass through the same process of dissolution as constitutes the historical evolution of the West?

The only answer to that possible today is this: If the Russian revolution becomes the signal for a proletarian revolution in the West, so that both complement each other, the present Russian common ownership of land may serve as the starting point for a communist development.

Friedrich Engels

London, January 21, 1882

At about the same date, a new Polish version appeared in Geneva.

Furthermore, a new Danish translation has appeared in the *Social-demokratisk Bibliothek*, Kjöbenhavn, 1885. Unfortunately, it is not quite complete; certain essential passages, which seem to have presented difficulties to the translator, have been omitted, and in addition there are signs of carelessness here and there, which are all the more unpleasantly conspicuous since the translation indicates that had the translator taken a little more pains he would have done an excellent piece of work.

Addenda

A new French version appeared in 1885 in *Le Socialiste* of Paris; it is the best published to date.

From this latter a Spanish version was published the same year, first in *El Socialista* of Madrid, and then reissued in pamphlet form: *Manifiesto del Partido Comunista* por Carlos Marx y F. Engels, Madrid, Administración de *El Socialista*, Hernán Cortés 8.

As a matter of curiosity I may also mention that in 1887 the manuscript of an Armenian translation was offered to a publisher in Constantinople. But the good man did not have the courage to publish something bearing the name of Marx, and suggested that the translator set down his own name as author, which the latter, however, declined.

After one and then another of the more or less inaccurate American translations had been repeatedly reprinted in England, an authentic version at last appeared in 1888. This was by my friend Samuel Moore, and we went through it together once more before it was sent to press. It is entitled: *Manifesto of the Communist Party,* by Karl Marx and Friedrich Engels. Authorized English Translation, edited and annotated by Friedrich Engels. 1888. London, William Reeves, 185 Fleet St., E. C. I have added some of the notes of that edition to the present one.

The *Manifesto* has had a history of its own.

131

Addenda

Greeted with enthusiasm, at the time of its appearance, by the then still not at all numerous vanguard of scientific socialism (as is proved by the translations mentioned in the first preface), it was soon forced into the background by the reaction that began with the defeat of the Paris workers in June, 1848, and was finally excommunicated "according to law" by the conviction of the Cologne Communists in November, 1852. With the disappearance from the public scene of the workers' movement that had begun with the February revolution, the *Manifesto*, too, passed into the background.

When the working class of Europe had again gathered sufficient strength for a new onslaught upon the power of the ruling classes, the International Workingmen's Association came into being. Its aim was to weld together into *one* huge army the whole militant working class of Europe and America. Therefore it could not *set out* from the principles laid down in the *Manifesto*. It was bound to have a program that would not shut the door on the English trade unions, the French, Belgian, Italian, and Spanish Proudhonists and the German Lassalleans.[2] This program—the preamble to the Rules

[2] Lassalle personally, to us, always acknowledged himself to be a "disciple" of Marx, and, as such, stood, of course, on the ground of the *Manifesto*. Matters were quite

of the International—was drawn up by Marx with a master hand acknowledged even by Bakunin and the anarchists. For the ultimate triumph of the ideas set forth in the *Manifesto,* Marx relied solely and exclusively upon the intellectual development of the working class, as it necessarily had to ensue from united action and discussion. The events and vicissitudes in the struggle against capital, the defeats even more than the successes, could not but demonstrate to the fighters the inadequacy hitherto of their universal panaceas and make their minds more receptive to a thorough understanding of the true conditions for the emancipation of the workers. And Marx was right. The working class of 1874, at the dissolution of the International, was altogether different from that of 1864, at its foundation. Proudhonism in the Latin countries and the specific Lassalleanism in Germany were dying out, and even the then archconservative English trade unions were gradually approaching the point where in 1887 the chairman of their Swansea Congress could say in their name, "Continental Socialism has lost its terrors for us." Yet by 1887 Continental socialism was almost exclusively the theory herald-

---

different with regard to those of his followers who did not go beyond his demand for producers' co-operatives supported by state credits and who divided the whole working class into supporters of state assistance and supporters of self-assistance. [*Note by Engels.*]

ed in the *Manifesto*. Thus, to a certain extent, the history of the *Manifesto* reflects the history of the modern working-class movement since 1848. At present it is doubtless the most widely circulated, the most international product of all socialist literature, the common program of many millions of workers of all countries from Siberia to California.

Nevertheless, when it appeared we could not have called it a *socialist* manifesto. In 1847 two kinds of people were considered Socialists. On the one hand were the adherents of the various utopian systems, notably the Owenites in England and the Fourierists in France, both of whom at that date had already dwindled to mere sects gradually dying out. On the other, the manifold types of social quacks who wanted to eliminate social abuses through their various universal panaceas and all kinds of patchwork, without hurting capital and profit in the least. In both cases, people who stood outside the labor movement and who looked for support rather to the "educated" classes. The section of the working class, however, which demanded a radical reconstruction of society, convinced that mere political revolutions were not enough, then called itself *Communist*. It was still a rough-hewn, only instinctive, and frequently somewhat crude communism. Yet it was powerful enough to bring into being two systems of utopian communism—in

France the "Icarian" communism of Cabet, and in Germany that of Weitling. Socialism in 1847 signified a bourgeois movement, communism, a working-class movement. Socialism was, on the Continent at least, quite respectable, whereas communism was the very opposite. And since we were very decidedly of the opinion as early as then that "the emancipation of the workers must be the act of the working class itself," we could have no hesitation as to which of the two names we should choose. Nor has it ever occurred to us since to repudiate it.

"Workingmen of all countries, unite!" But few voices responded when we proclaimed these words to the world forty-two years ago, on the eve of the first Paris revolution in which the proletariat came out with demands of its own. On September 28, 1864, however, the proletarians of most of the Western European countries joined hands in the International Workingmen's Association of glorious memory. True, the International itself lived only nine years. But that the eternal union of the proletarians of all countries created by it is still alive and lives stronger than ever, there is no better witness than this day. Because today, as I write these lines, the European and American proletariat is reviewing its fighting forces, mobilized for the first time, mobilized as *one* army, under *one* flag, for *one* immediate aim: the standard eight-hour working day, to be established by legal enactment, as proclaimed by the Geneva Congress of the International in 1866, and again by the Paris Workers' Congress in 1889. And today's spectacle will open the eyes of the capitalists and landlords of all countries to the fact that today the workingmen of all countries are united indeed.

If only Marx were still by my side to see this with his own eyes!

Friedrich Engels

London, May 1, 1890

Preface to the Polish Edition of 1892

THE fact that a new Polish edition of the *Communist Manifesto* has become necessary gives rise to various thoughts.

First of all, it is noteworthy that of late the *Manifesto* has become an index, as it were, of the development of large-scale industry on the European continent. In proportion as large-scale industry expands in a given country, the demand grows among the workers of that country for enlightenment regarding their position as the working class in relation to the possessing classes, the socialist movement spreads among them and the demand for the *Manifesto* increases. Thus, not only the state of the labor movement but also the degree of development of large-scale industry can be measured with fair accuracy in every country by the number of copies of the *Manifesto* circulated in the language of that country.

Accordingly, the new Polish edition indicates a decided progress of Polish industry. And there can be no doubt whatever that this progress since the previous edition published ten years ago has actually taken place. Russian Poland, Congress Poland, has become the big industrial region of the Russian Empire. Whereas Russian large-scale industry is scattered sporadically—a part round the Gulf of Finland, another in the center (Moscow and Vladimir), a third along the coasts of the Black and Azov seas, and still others elsewhere—Polish industry has been packed into a relatively small area and enjoys both the advantages and the disadvantages arising from such concentration. The competing Russian manufacturers acknowledged the advantages when they demanded protective tariffs against Poland, in spite of their ardent desire to transform the Poles into Russians. The disadvantages—for the Polish manufacturers and the Russian government —are manifest in the rapid spread of socialist ideas among the Polish workers and in the growing demand for the *Manifesto*.

But the rapid development of Polish industry, outstripping that of Russia, is in its turn a new proof of the inexhaustible vitality of the Polish people and a new guarantee of its impending national restoration. And the restoration of an independent strong Poland is a matter which concerns not only the Poles but all of us. A sincere international collaboration of the European nations is possible only if each of these nations is fully autonomous in its own house. The Revolution of 1848, which under the banner of the proletariat, after all, merely let the proletarian fighters do the work of the bourgeoisie, also secured the independence of Italy, Germany, and Hungary through its testamentary executors, Louis Bonaparte and Bismarck; but Poland, which since 1792 had done more for the revolution than all these three together, was left to its own resources when it succumbed in 1863 to a tenfold greater Russian force. The nobility could neither maintain nor regain Polish independence; today, to the bourgeoisie, this independence is, to say the least, immaterial. Nevertheless, it is a necessity for the harmonious collaboration of the European nations. It can be gained only by the young Polish proletariat, and in its hands it is secure. For the workers of all the rest of Europe need the independence of Poland just as much as the Polish workers themselves.

Friedrich Engels

London, February 10, 1892

Preface to the Italian Edition of 1893

To the Italian Reader

PUBLICATION of the *Manifesto of the Communist Party* coincided, one may say, with March 18, 1848, the day of the revolutions in Milan and Berlin, which were armed uprisings of the two nations situated in the center, the one, of the continent of Europe, the other, of the Mediterranean; two nations until then enfeebled by division and internal strife, and thus fallen under foreign domination. While Italy was subject to the Emperor of Austria, Germany underwent the yoke, not less effective though more indirect, of the tsar of all the Russias. The consequences of March 18, 1848, freed both Italy and Germany from this disgrace; if from 1848 to 1871 these two great nations were reconstituted and somehow again put on their own, it was, as Karl Marx used to say, because the men who suppressed the Revolution of 1848 were, nevertheless, its testamentary executors in spite of themselves.

Everywhere that revolution was the work of the working class; it was the latter that built the barricades and paid with its lifeblood. Only the Paris workers, in overthrowing the government, had the very definite intention of overthrowing the bourgeois regime. But conscious though they were of the fatal antagonism existing between their own class and the bourgeoisie, still, neither the economic progress of the country nor the intellectual development of the mass of French workers had as yet reached the stage which would have made a social reconstruction possible. In the final analysis, therefore, the fruits of the revolution were reaped by the capitalist class. In the other countries, in Italy, in Germany, in Austria, the workers, from the very outset, did nothing but raise the bourgeoisie to power. But in any country the rule of the bourgeoisie is impossible without national independence. Therefore, the Revolution of 1848 had to bring in its train the unity and autonomy of the nations that had lacked them up to then: Italy, Germany, Hungary. Poland will follow in turn.

Thus, if the Revolution of 1848 was not a socialist revolution, it paved the way, prepared the ground for the latter. Through the impetus given to large-scale industry in all countries, the bourgeois regime during the last forty-five years has everywhere created a numerous, concentrated, and powerful proletariat. It has thus raised, to use the language of the *Manifesto,* its own grave-diggers. Without restoring autonomy and unity to each nation, it will be impossible to achieve the international union of the proletariat, or the peaceful and intelligent co-operation of these nations toward common aims. Just imagine joint international action by the Italian, Hungarian, German, Polish, and Russian workers under the political conditions preceding 1848!

The battles fought in 1848 were thus not fought in vain. Nor have the forty-five years separating us from that revolutionary epoch passed to no purpose. The fruits are ripening, and all I wish is that the publication of this Italian translation may augur as well for the victory of the Italian proletariat as the publication of the original did for the international revolution.

The *Manifesto* does full justice to the revolutionary part played by capitalism in the past. The first capitalist nation was Italy. The close of the feudal Middle Ages and the opening of the modern capitalist era are marked by a colossal figure: an Italian, Dante, both the last poet of the Middle Ages and the first poet of modern times. Today, as in 1300, a new historical era is approaching. Will Italy give us the new Dante, who will mark the hour of birth of this new, proletarian era?

Friedrich Engels

London, February, 1, 1893